THE WRONG CALAMITY

CALAMITY

A Memoir

MARSHA JACOBSON

Printed in the United States of America

Hardcover ISBN: 978-1-959096-92-4
Paperback ISBN: 978-1-959096-93-1
Ebook ISBN: 978-1-959096-94-8
Library of Congress Control Number: 2023943850

DartFrog Plus
A division of DartFrog Books
4697 Main Street
Manchester Center, VT 05255

PRAISE FOR THE WRONG CALAMITY

"Courageous...an affecting, personal exploration of toxic relationships."

—Kirkus Reviews

"Jacobson's debut is an elegant, engaging account of her life as a wife and mother facing a harrowing marriage, then as a single parent and eventual successful business executive.

Jacobson's excellent storytelling skills make the memoir riveting. She plunges us straight into the heart of things right from the beginning and is able to maintain this steady pace through the book. At the same time, the narrative is thoughtful and reflective when the story demands. Unpredictable and domineering, Peter is the most interesting character in the book, though for negative reasons. So is Judge Samuel. Marsha's second husband Jay, meanwhile, endures the far-reaching consequences of childhood abuse, sensitive material that Jacobson handles with insight and empathy. Minnie and Julia, Marsha's grandmothers, are incredibly strong and empathetic women who with their kindness and help support their neglected grandchild.

Jacobson's career takes her to fascinating places, such as Mattel headquarters in Japan, and she captures them and their cultures with nuance and welcome bursts of wit. She addresses work challenges and the several ways in which she tackled them. Her obvious passion for her chosen career is evident in these anecdotes. Jacobson's never-say-die attitude, her immense love for her two girls, and her strong narrative skills make this memoir an absorbing and rewarding read."

—BookLife

"Marsha Jacobson's existence has definitely never been a bed of roses. When she was young, her painful lack of self-confidence due to a weight problem led her into a marriage with an abusive, overpowering man, who harassed her for years by taking her to court after she broke free of him. She raised two daughters, put herself through Harvard business school and gradually built a successful career while battling serious health problems. She fell deeply in love and married a second time but did not find lasting happiness....What's refreshingly different about this memoir, however, is that Jacobson, rather than dwelling upon how much she suffered, gives us the facts rather briskly and then goes on to write about what interests her far more—the resourceful and courageous ways she coped with one crisis after another. The result is fascinating and compelling reading."

—Joyce Johnson,
author of the prizewinning memoir *Minor Characters*

"Marsha Jacobson's *The Wrong Calamity* is a courageously written story of a courageously lived life. She takes us inside unexpected stress and pain to renewed hope with humane clarity."

—Walter Bode,
former editor-in-chief of Grove Press and
senior editor at Harcourt Publishing

"From her re-entry into dating and the snafus that led to new realizations about those she chose and her moral and ethical foundations to business and personal growth choices, Jacobson creates a powerful story of calamity, discovery, and change. This will serve as an inspiration (and road map) to other women facing similar conundrums.

Libraries and readers seeking stories of not just escape from abuse, but considerations of the financial, psychology, and social influences on their evolution, will find *The Wrong Calamity* enlightening, revealing, and hard to put down."

—Midwest Book Review

"Exploring super difficult topics, the author has courageously penned her life story while throwing light on how her traumas shaped her and her relationships... It takes bravery to share such a story & immense skill to make the reader feel the story."

—Mowgli With a Book, Instagram

"Heart-wrenching, inspiring and thought-provoking."

—Read to Write, Instagram

"Readers who enjoy stories of everyday women overcoming adversity will find Jacobson's story to be a worthwhile read."

—Purrfect Pages, Instagram

"Marsha really left it all on the pages in The Wrong Calamity. A lot can be learned from her words."

—Joanna's Bookshelf, Instagram

"This book is written in a very conversational manner and is easy to get into. Jacobson is talented in so many ways—music, academia and intelligence, career performance, and more. The book shows how women devalue their gifts and give too much time and effort to failings."

—Audrey Oaks Reads Everything, Instagram

"Recommended to those who like memoirs and stories of empowerment."

—Books.Cats.Travel.Food., Instagram

"A well written memoir that tells her story as if I'm sitting down with a friend and catching up on life updates. Jacobson has a wonderful way of telling her story."

—Nurse Bookie, Instagram

"My heart broke for this woman reading her story, it is heartbreaking and empowering at the same time. She did not give up, she did not crumble, she survived and persevered through more than any woman should have to live through. If you are a non-fiction lover and you are looking for a memoir to read, this one is worth picking up."

—Reading With Nicole, Instagram

"Simultaneously heartbreaking and hopeful."

—Bayering with Freshman, Instagram

AUTHOR'S NOTE

This is a true story. Names and some identifying characteristics have been changed to respect the privacy of certain individuals. These changes in no way affect the integrity of this book.

For my daughters and grandmothers

−1−
A WIZ THERE IS

I WAS BORN IN THE WHOOSH of baby boomers at Lafayette, Indiana's Saint Elizabeth's hospital, where the wards were named with Bible references and the maternity ward was labeled Immaculate Conception. I was a preemie, weighing less than five pounds, and when a nurse introduced me to my father, he said, to her horror, "Last night I ate a chicken bigger than that."

He was a provocative guy, quick to argue with his bosses, and we moved from place to place as he lost and found jobs. We were living in a New Jersey suburb flush with TV Dinners, Mr. Potato Heads, and other new-fashioned things when bad news came from the Bronx. My father's father, my grandpa Max, had had a stroke and could no longer run his knitwear factory. His wife, my grandma Minnie, was the right person for this emergency. Arriving in America at thirteen, she'd found a job in a sweater factory as a cleanup girl, securing dropped stitches and such, and from there had gone on to bigger jobs in bigger factories. Now she converted the office into a little bedsit and made sure Max had a hot lunch, a daily nap, and full respect while she ran the place from a desk at the foot of his daybed. Eventually, she brought in my father and taught him the business, ending his job-hopping.

One summer day, for what would turn out to be the last time, I skated up and down our driveway until I knew the farm hands would be gone and I could finally go to the flower farm near my school. There, I lay on my back in the pansies and framed clusters of clouds with my outstretched hands. Velvety petals brushed the sides of my face, and if I turned my head just a little, the pansies held me with their gentle eyes. Back home, my parents were screaming and storming out of rooms, but here there was peace.

Early the next morning, my mother yanked me out of sleep by my shoulders and pushed me against the wall. Two enormous men stood behind her.

"Who are they?" I screamed. "Where's Daddy?"

"Daddy's at work," she screamed back. "Get out of the way!"

Crouching low in my yellow baby-dolls, trying to hide my naked legs and hints of breasts, I sobbed into my knees as the men carried away my bed. Their truck took off with everything we owned, and a car pulled up to drive us to the airport. My mother was taking us back to Indiana, where her people were. My brother Craig was two and ecstatic to be on a plane, but I panicked.

"I'm supposed to be at Adrienne's! We're going skating!"

"You'll skate in Indiana," my mother said, strapping me in.

"What about sixth grade?"

"They have sixth grades in Indiana!"

How would I return my library books? Who would water the plants by the porch? What about my friends? Question after question, until, finally, I asked the two that frightened me most. "How will Daddy find us? And Grandma Minnie?"

"Your father will know everything soon enough," my mother said. "And you can forget about Minnie. Now turn that sad face of yours away from me."

I turned my sad face to the cloud-filled window and silently grieved my New Jersey life, needing more than ever my Grandma Minnie, who, I knew, loved me and would know what to do.

In Indiana, my mother's old friends swooped her up into the bridge and mahjong circuit, and the family embraced our return. Uncle Allan gave us a car, and Grandma Julia bought us a house. Occasionally I played with my Indiana cousins, but mostly I stayed home, waiting for my father. As the summer went on and still he didn't come, I pictured him searching for me, running from house to house and banging on doors in all the wrong places.

"You have to write and tell him where we are," I nagged my mother.

"He knows exactly where we are," she said. "He's known since we got here."

All that time I'd waited for him, and he'd never even set out. He'd later say he phoned constantly and she hung up on him. She'd say he never called. Who knows? The one thing I do know is that back then I saw myself as my mother did: nothing worth caring about; and as my father did: nothing worth thinking about. And I thought that somehow I'd wronged both of them.

It was spring. My sixth-grade teacher was coming to our house to talk to my mother, and I'd stood up all afternoon so my skirt wouldn't wrinkle. I flew to the door when the bell rang, but my mother pushed past me and said, "Come in, Mr. Dalton. Have a seat."

Practically whispering, I asked if I could sit with him. "Please do," he said, and he patted the spot next to him on the couch. He told my mother I read like a ninth-grader and my arithmetic was the best in the school. Then he turned and winked at me. My face got hot. I wasn't sure if I should wink back, and I hiked up my shoulders and looked at my lap. That's when I heard my mother's voice.

"If she's so good at everything, why's her room such a mess?"

My breath stopped. If I inhaled, my chest would crack.

Mr. Dalton made a noise in his throat and said, in a tight voice I hadn't heard before, "Well, that's just normal at this age."

"Not as messy as hers, it isn't. You can't imagine."

A terrible, grasping thing in need of succor clutched at my stomach. After Mr. Dalton left, I sneaked into the kitchen and ate bread. A lot of bread. As I squeezed slices into little balls and crammed them into my mouth, I silently cried out to my mother, Didn't you hear? I read like a ninth-grader!

Years later, when my own daughter was grown, both her father and mine would act up on a special day of hers, and she'd tell me, "You're the only one I can rely on not to embarrass me." As soon as she said it, I knew how I'd learned not to, but to say I was grateful for the lesson is a step too far.

At Jefferson High School, under a banner that said, "Jeff Excels in Many Areas," my guidance counselor sat slumped over papers on his desk, head in hands, and didn't look up when I arrived to get my SAT scores. "Such a shame," he was muttering.

"I'm so sorry," he said, head still down, "but you're going to have a hard life," as though the papers were lab results and he, a doctor. "People with normal scores, when a problem comes up, they see only one or two options. But the ones with high scores like these"—so now I knew I'd done well, but was well bad?—"with these scores, they see too many choices. They torture themselves."

One day I'd know this was nutty, but back then I was a kid who took him to heart. "What should I do?" I asked.

He answered, sadly, "There's nothing you *can* do."

The following year, this same guidance counselor told me I had the grades for automatic acceptance to Purdue, our hometown school, and left it at that. I interpreted this to mean that all I had to do was, well, I wasn't sure, phone Purdue or something, but my rabbi, Steve Weisberg, and his wife, DeeDee, told me, "You should get away. Why don't you go to Brandeis?" which is where they'd gone. I applied there, and, to please them, I desperately wanted to get in, but Brandeis didn't respond.

On a perfect May night, celebrating my eighteenth birthday with friends and family, I made my birthday wish out loud: "I just want the Brandeis letter to come." My mother lowered her fork and sighed deeply, her eyes tragic as a silent screen star's. "It came," she said. "A month ago. You got in, but they didn't give you enough money. You can't go."

I cried for days. My mother sighed for a while, then got on with other things. I called my father, who said, "You? Got into Brandeis?" and would pay nothing.

"Is everybody crazy around here?" said Grandma Julia, and she wrote the check.

When I left for Brandeis, it didn't occur to my mother or father to go with me, and for my part, I didn't know that's what parents did. I flew to Boston alone and took a cab to the campus. On my solitary walk to my dorm, the hilly prettiness of the place, with its low brick buildings snugged into stands of trees, stopped me still. I'd imagined Indiana-flat stretches of imperious buildings and huge parking lots right on the streets of town, like Purdue. But this was a campus with a single entrance, a cozy white information booth, and a gently curving drive into a world small enough to wrap your arms around.

As I approached my dorm, I watched clusters of my new classmates and their families exchange breezy greetings. They looked so comfortable, jaunty even, while I felt like I'd slipped through an invisible membrane and emerged there by accident. My stomach clenched. I had nothing in common with anyone there. My arms bulged in my sleeves, and, with familiar desperation, I felt my skirt ride up my thighs with each step I took. These students were lithe and buoyant. They would sail through Brandeis. But I weighed two hundred pounds and would sink to the bottom and get mudbound.

No one there had heard of Jefferson High or knew that the Jeff Bronchos were the Indiana state high school basketball champs. I'd counted on that championship as a conversation starter, but now, with quizzical looks telling me not to mention it again, I was high and dry with nothing to say after hello. There I was, at a liberal school in the 1960s and only vaguely aware of what everyone was talking about—Mandela, Vietnam,

Mississippi. These kids went to museums, read more than one newspaper, knew the names of governors of states they didn't live in. "Of course I know the Beatles!" I said, insulted when it came to light that I didn't know the Rolling Stones.

My financial aid package required me to earn a hefty amount on my own, and though I waitressed in the cafeteria, punched IBM cards in the computer room, and loaded tapes in the language lab, I still had to find one more job.

"Check with Peter," said a sophomore. "He's a wizard."

"Go straight to Peter," my dorm advisor said. "Skip the Work-Study Office."

So I went to find this Peter. He was an assistant dean in charge of special projects, and he worked out of a dorm room in a quad at the far edge of campus. A single bed in the corner was the only sign that this was his home as well as his office, but it was piled so high with papers, I doubted he ever got into it. A current ran through him, a charge from some mysterious source that seemed to make sleep nonessential. Rumor was he never slept at all, and if that was a myth, probably he himself started it. Certainly he encouraged it.

He was six years older than me, but I thought he was even older. A cartoonist would have had fun with his scraggle-fringed baldness, wrinkled trousers, and clip-on bow ties. He was large and pear-shaped, led with his belly, and moved on out-turned feet with much swaying and bobbing. But he was fast as a silverfish. He could cross the room and open the door by the second beat of knock-knock, then get back across to grab the phone before the first ring ended. He was always in motion on a call, pacing around furniture and a student or two who might be waiting to see him. As he tacked and jibed, his beloved fifty-foot phone cord wrapped itself around the floor lamp, the chairs, the hapless students, and his own hips. Every few minutes, he'd pirouette to unwrap his body, then retrace his route to give himself enough cord to pace again.

We wouldn't have the internet for another thirty years, but we had Peter. Off the top of his head, he could tell you the date of the next eclipse, the best way to get from Boston to Lahore, and the show times of every movie playing in Boston. He was a music buff, a man who loved cities and knew how to live in them, and, most of all, a transportation nut who flew to foreign countries just to ride the subways. It turned out he needed an assistant, and he hired me that afternoon.

To me, he was dazzling. I saw him as part of my education, a type of person I hadn't known existed. This he was, but he was also a man who recognized those he could reel in. He became my new planet, and I became a moon in his orbit. There were five other moons, all guys. I thought they were sophisticated and discerning, validation that to be in Peter's orbit was to be someone special, but later, even before they outgrew him, I understood that their luster was less remarkable than I'd first thought, just an urbanity I hadn't encountered back in Indiana. By then, though, I was firmly in Peter's gravitational pull.

The six of us would go with him on outings that he insisted we keep secret. For that matter, he ordered us not to let on even that we knew him. If we saw him around school, he nodded curtly and kept moving. Among ourselves, we exchanged almost imperceptible darts of connection, like secret handshakes, but fleeting. We thought we were his friends, but we were more like subjects. Where did he go when he wasn't with us? What did he read? Did he watch TV?

Have a family? Friends would have chatted about such things, but Peter, never. If one of us slipped and asked even, "How was your weekend?" he'd rear back and send his eyebrows skyward in a clear "No comment."

When Peter beckoned, we gathered on a little-traveled road near campus to be whisked in his station wagon to a destination unknown. We could find ourselves at an unpublicized lecture at Harvard, on a private tour of the Boston Flower Exchange, or in the Blue Hills observing a rare night-sky phenomenon through a telescope he drew from his trunk.

One night, he pulled up in front of an out-of-the-way ice cream shop a few towns over, the only lit spot on a shuttered street. "They invent all their flavors here," he said, "and they make each batch by hand." With a magician's pizzazz, he raised one arm and poof!—a waitress appeared with seven scoops of ice cream he'd pre-ordered. "It's miraculous," he declared. "Found nowhere else on earth!" Never mind that we might have wanted chocolate. We ate.

Even Nathan, a sweet, peaceable flutist in our fellowship, gave in after Peter stood firm and refused to reveal the ingredients. Suddenly we were rushing Nathan to the hospital. Under Peter's spell, he'd eaten unidentified green fruity ice cream despite a severe honeydew allergy.

Maybe that was when the guys started pulling away from Peter, but perhaps their retreat began a little later, the night he took the station wagon from thirty to forty to sixty on a bumpy dirt road. Thrown around the two rear seats in those pre-seatbelt days, they screamed at him to stop the car. Instead, he went to eighty, laughing a movie villain bwa-ha-ha and leaning forward, elbows out, chest to the steering wheel. Beside him in the front, I was terrified, but I yelled back to them, "It's okay! He's controlling it!" What the hell was I thinking?

Over the next couple of years, Peter became more secretive, more uncompromising, and inexplicably animated. Still, as the guys peeled off, I thought, Too bad for them, and I felt special. By my junior year, I was the only one still with him in the station wagon, riding with my man, my crazy man.

We weren't exactly like Henry Higgins and Eliza Doolittle, but we weren't exactly different, either. He took me to New Hampshire for the foliage and to Salem for the witches. He took me to *Don Giovanni*, my first opera, walking me through the libretto ahead of time and telling me what to listen for in the major arias. In small, spare restaurants, he ordered exotic dishes and showed me how to eat them. These out-of-the-way places served customers homesick for their native lands. The menus were written on blackboards in foreign languages, and the servers spoke no English, but they beamed when he walked in, and they knew his name.

The summer before my senior year, Peter left Brandeis over a disagreement with the dean and started teaching in the Boston public school system. For weeks, I brooded over whether he'd stop calling me. If he did, it wouldn't rightly be a breakup—we weren't rightly a couple—but it would certainly be a disruption of the natural order. There was an established choreography for these things. The man led, and after a certain number of spins you became a couple or ended the dance. Though we were long overdue for resolution, Peter hadn't declared a position, and things were playing out more like having a crush on a teacher than having a boyfriend. We didn't even hold hands. I was confused, but also afraid to push.

I almost cried the first time he called, and to my relief, he kept calling. On we went, like an old habit, and I was spared any serious thinking. Nothing had changed. Twice a week or so, he'd call after dinner and tell me where to meet him. No matter what I was doing, I'd drop it and go, telling myself that whatever he'd planned would be worth later staying up all night to finish my homework.

At the end of these evenings, he'd turn into an abandoned driveway near school. Suddenly he'd be impatient. With the engine still running and no real goodbye, I'd slip out and walk briskly toward campus, like a criminal dropped far from the crime by the getaway car.

The only person Peter said I could talk to about him was Ed Simon, a microbiology professor back at Purdue. I'd babysat his kids from the time I was fourteen, and one summer I worked in his lab, anesthetizing fruit flies. He'd once asked what I was studying in high school and was so appalled by my answers, he started tutoring me in science and history when he drove me home from babysitting. He was hardly systematic. One time he talked about Napoleon; another time, asparagus pee. His lessons would always be longer than the ride, and we'd park outside my house until my next-door neighbor flashed his porch light on and off, shocked that I was dallying so long in a car with a man.

Ed was a fatherly friend, and at Brandeis I often dropped coins into a payphone and talked to him about Peter. Even with Ed, though, someone wholly in my court, I left out the parts that weren't storybook and put a gloss on anything that might paint Peter as romantic.

One evening, during my senior year, Peter drove me back to campus after a concert, and instead of leaving the engine running for me to jump out, he turned it off.

"So," he said, "what do you think about all this?"

"All what?"

"You and me."

I'd been waiting a long time for this, but now that it had come, I felt my stomach clench and heard my pulse beat in my ears. "You and me?" I asked. "What do you mean?"

But Peter just looked straight ahead, lips clamped.

He'd punted to me, and I punted to Ed Simon.

"Ed says I might be in love with you," I told him.

"I might be in love with you too," he answered. But then he just sat there, still looking through the windshield.

Finally I said, "So are we a couple?"

"We're a couple," he said, "but let's live with it privately for a while," and—my signal to hop out—he started the engine.

− 2 −

QUICKSAND

He might say, "in the spring we'll go to the Blue Hills," and, with a coquettishness that today makes me sad, I'd ask, "Is that a proposal?"

"That is *not* a proposal," he'd answer, loving it when I scrunched my face and shook my fist in mock frustration.

Whatever he suggested, I, Old Faithful, would say, "Is that a proposal?" It was his favorite joke. I was the one who'd started it, for no good reason, and soon it was a thing I couldn't snuff out. In time it made me nervous, though I didn't probe the feeling, and when I stopped asking the question, he'd answer it anyway. "Let's go see my grandparents," he'd say, "and no, that is not a proposal."

The summer after I graduated, we went to Canada for a vacation. We were walking along a stretch of brambly, shrubby sand by a lake near Montreal, and in the hot sun I slipped off my shoes and waded in to mid-calf. Almost immediately a woman in a house across the street came out on her porch, waving her arms and yelling, "Quicksand! There's quicksand in there! Get out!"

Only then did I realize I had sunk in ankle-deep and there was a hungry pull on my feet.

"See if you can find a branch or something to pull me out with," I called to Peter.

"You got yourself into this," he said. He turned his head slowly to the left, then to the right, then folded his arms on his chest. "Anyway, there's nothing."

So stunned I couldn't think, I forced myself to focus on my feet and didn't answer. With slow, careful moves I managed to work myself free, and soon we were walking again. My calves were itchy with drying mud. There was grit in my sandals. Adrenaline and some contradictory force battled in my body. The adrenaline ordered my muscles to keep fighting, though I'd left the quicksand behind. The other thing seeped through me like anesthesia, shutting down the shock of Peter's indifference.

Suddenly he jumped ahead of me with four fast giant steps, whirled around to face me, and, arms spread out to block my way, said, "How would you like to grow old together?"

My stomach churned. With utter clarity, my mind saw an elderly couple sitting dully on matching club chairs, saying nothing, not looking at each other, continents apart in a dark, spiritless living room.

"And yes!" he exulted. "That's a proposal!"

Hands on hips and smiling triumphantly, he waited for my answer, but I was stuck in that lifeless living room and couldn't speak. Soon he grew jittery, and I felt I had to rescue him.

"Yes," I said.

"You don't look happy," he complained, but then carried on as though I did.

I'd later tell myself I'd been too young, too inexperienced, that there was no way I could have foreseen what would come. But that wasn't true. What were those two old people in the forlorn living room if not a picture speaking a thousand words? What was "You don't look happy," if not the whole story? And for crying out loud—quicksand? Harbingers were everywhere, trying to get me to know what I knew, but because I had no idea what to do with the knowledge, I ignored them.

And here's something even worse. In the instant before I said yes, I saw, clearly, an image of myself in a coffin. I actually heard the sibilant exhale of the pistons and the decisive click of the lock as the lid closed on me.

"It's over," I said to myself, meaning I'm not sure what, and to him I said again, "Yes."

It would be years before I understood where the images of the living room and the coffin came from, but it's inescapable that when it mattered, for just an instant, I knew this marriage would nail me into a very bad box, and immediately I was resigned to it. The sorry truth is, I was relieved to have things settled.

— 3 —

WALRUS

THERE'S A PHOTO OF ME IN fourth grade, sweetly plump and clearly feeling pretty, holding my skirt out wide and about to twirl. By sixth grade, my new height hasn't kept up with my new weight. By eighth grade I'm undeniably fat; my humiliating gym suit barely buttons, and I can't run around the perimeter of the gym no matter how many times the gym teacher makes me try while the other girls stand and watch.

That year, my worldview was still mercifully unformed. I didn't yet realize that most people thought my body said everything they needed to know about me, and I suffered mostly about my very wrong clothes.

Back then, girls wore belted shirtwaists or straight skirts with tucked-in blouses, but there were none of those in my size. Today, you can find anything, even bikinis, in large sizes, but I had only a local store's "Women's Department"—really just an unattended rack or two back by the fire stairs, with big, square dresses like refrigerator boxes.

Only one of the twelve hundred students at Jefferson High School was obese. I was that kid. By then I understood that the bigger I got, the more invisible I became. And I was very big. You know those children's worksheets? Apple, pear, banana, walrus . . . which one doesn't belong? I was walrus. In the speech team and chorus photos in the school lobby, I took up the space of two. Whenever I walked past them, I just wanted to scissor myself out, trophies and all. Everybody knew who I was, but not because of my singing voice, my wins at public speaking competitions, or my bylines in the school paper. I was the fat kid. It might as well have been my name.

Imperceptibly, I myself came to see only my weight. "You're not fat," Worth said, often. I know you think you are, but you're not."

Ah, Worth. My best friend then and now. We met in sophomore German, on the day Frau Marquart asked the class to translate the sentence *Wenigstens gibt es Reis*.

"'Please give us rice'?"

"'Wenigstens is rich'?"

One after another, students went down guessing.

"It means 'At least there's rice,'" said Frau Marquart, visibly struggling to keep her frustration in check. "*Wenigstens gibt es*! It's an idiom! It means 'At least there's'!"

She turned to the blackboard, and Worth, one row over and one seat back, tossed a note onto my desk. "Wenigstens gibt es only five more minutes in here," it said. I grinned and looked her way, but she was unimpeachably concentrating on her German book. We hadn't spoken before, but, as if it were planned, the two of us met in the hall after class and started a conversation that has never stopped. "Wenigstens gibt es Reis" is still our shorthand for "Things could be worse."

Forty years later, when I wanted to know if I'd been as fat in high school as I remembered, I called Worth.

"I'll dig out my yearbooks tonight," she said. "I think you'll be surprised. You were tall, a little large, but not like you think. Narrow shoulders, a small waist. What was different about you was the way you dressed. I always felt sorry for you, wearing those clothes."

Her email soon followed, with photos of yearbook pages attached. The subject line was "Flabbergasted." I'd remembered correctly.

Junior year was when all my friends started dating, and I was left behind. Some went out with a series of guys. Some had fairly-steadies. The luckiest had actual boyfriends who gave them their chunky class rings to wear, made small enough for petite fingers with coils and coils of conspicuous, hairy yarn wrapped around the shanks. In all of high school, I would have no boyfriend or even a date, except for one disastrous time when mothers colluded.

My next-door neighbor was a creep called Junior whose mother was beside herself because he hung out with the bad boys and couldn't get a date. She made him ask me to a dance, and my mother made me accept. I argued with my mother for days, but I never had a chance.

"I have nothing to wear!"

"And whose fault is that?"

"Everybody hates him! I can't be seen with him!"

"You're not someone who can be choosy!"

The night of the dance, my friend Ginny showed up in poufy pink with ruffles. Marianne was in blue with sequins. I was in a schoolmarmy thing in brown checked wool—a tailored shirtwaist with buttons, a belt, and a pocket with a fake handkerchief sticking out.

As soon as we entered the ballooned and streamered gym, Junior abandoned me and smirked around with his pomaded, thumbs-tucked-behind-belt-buckle buddies. For two hours, until his dad came to get us, I hid in the bathroom or walked the perimeter in my matronly dress, looking like a middle-aged chaperone who'd ridiculously put on a wrist corsage.

The next day, I ate my lunch hiding in a bathroom stall, unable to face the dance talk in the cafeteria. As it was, I'd already become a sideliner there, where most of the talk was about the other girls' weekend dates or quests to get one. Ultimately, I volunteered to be the soloist at services at my synagogue, attended mostly by old friends of my grandmother, so that I could answer questions about my own weekend plans with a wistful, "I have to work."

Our old rabbi left, and a young new rabbi, Rabbi Steve Weisberg, arrived. After several weeks, he pulled me aside. "It's great having you here," he said, "but you should be going out more with your friends. If you ever want to skip, I'll cover for you."

I was too embarrassed to tell him I had no weekend friends, and I didn't have the presence of mind to just say thank you. Instead, I protested too much and felt like an idiot. On the way home I bought three doughnuts and ate them in the car.

And now, five years later, here I was, fatter than ever and engaged to be married.

Peter took me to an expensive restaurant in Montreal to celebrate our engagement. I acted happy, and in no time, I believed my own performance. While we ate, he told me he'd be planning our honeymoon by himself and it would be a surprise. Fine, I thought. Let him do it. He loves that stuff.

But the honeymoon was the least of it. For years I'd dreamed of casually flashing a diamond. I wanted to check out venues and size up caterers, to deliberate between beef Wellington and coq au vin. I wanted announcements in the *Boston Globe* and the *Lafayette Journal & Courier* and even a fraught weekend working out table assignments. But Peter wouldn't hear of it. He couldn't stand the hoopla, he said, and he didn't want other people weighing in. He wouldn't let anyone, not even his family, celebrate his birthday, he reminded me. And that was true. I was marrying a man whose birthday I didn't know.

Peter was adamant that we not tell our families about our engagement until three days before the wedding, not tell our friends until we were back from our honeymoon. No caterer, no photographer, no hall, just a simple ceremony with an unknown rabbi, since his family rabbi might spill the beans.

"Small and simple," he said. "Just immediate family. Get some wine, buy a cake. Done. If we're going to be married, this is how it has to be."

He threw down the gauntlet, and I let it lie there. The images of the coffin and the couple in the dark living room hovered tentatively on the edge of my consciousness, but I brushed them away. Wedding details were unimportant in the grand scheme of things, I told myself.

I gave in on everything except the store-bought cake. I would bake a family heirloom for the occasion: my grandmother Julia's nine-inch-high yellow and white marbled Sunshine Angel Cake.

When we got back from Canada, Peter dropped me at my apartment and went on to his parents' house, where he'd lived since he left Brandeis. Lest we be seen in a Boston store, we bought rings from a random jeweler in Providence, and Peter whisked them into his pocket to hold until the wedding. He found a rabbi with no ties to either of us, and we settled on a wedding date six months away. Peter would be twenty-eight and I'd be twenty-two, too old to undermine myself so readily. "We were all like that back then," says a friend today, which may or may not be true and certainly is no comfort.

A few weeks later, I started teaching fifth grade at the Dearborn School, a Boston elementary school where Peter was the science teacher. He insisted we not tell our colleagues even that we knew each other outside of work, and I went along with it. A friendly and open person, little by little I'd come to lead a secretive life.

My grandmother Minnie and I had been reunited shortly before I started seventh grade, when the terms of my parents' divorce were settled. My summers had been allocated to my father, and he'd reallocated them to Minnie so he could go to work. She was the one person I took all my doubts to, and she always knew what to do. Certainly I should have told her about Peter, but I didn't. Because she always knew what to do.

Worth was the other person I might have confided in. She was back in Indiana, just graduated from Purdue, and, with email far in the future and long-distance calls expensive, we kept in touch with postcards and letters. I didn't know even how to begin explaining my situation, and I procrastinated writing until, eventually, I forgot my intention. Then I got a letter from her, giving me the perfect opening. She'd gotten married. "And here I am," she wrote, "in my very own apartment, looking at my very own dish drainer."

I flew back to Indiana to see her and meet her husband, expecting her to be somehow more grown up in her wifedom. Even as I rang her bell, I felt awkward and out of my league. Worth's grad-student husband was in class, and as the two of us settled in to talk, she produced a couple of glasses and a bottle of wine that cost not the usual $3 but an astounding $20, about $160 today.

"I figured this is our chance to see if expensive wines are really different," she said as she poured.

She swirled her glass around, inhaled deeply to take in the aroma, and sipped. I waited for her proclamation.

"Oh no!" she said.

"Not good?"

"Delicious. I really hoped there wouldn't be a difference."

"Wenigstens gibt es Reis," we said in unison.

In the face of her ease with her marriage and her courage to experiment extravagantly, I felt hopelessly small-town, even though I was the one who lived in Boston and she was still in Lafayette. She seemed so grown up, so poised. I couldn't think of a way to make my relationship with Peter sound reasonable, and so I took the news of my engagement back home with me, still a secret. What a crazy business that was.

Only when I went to buy my wedding dress did I venture out of the shadows and into the light of bridal glory. I told the clerk I was getting married, the first time I'd said it out loud. For a quick, stolen moment I basked in her much-practiced, squealy congratulations, and then I got down to the task at hand.

"Something nice, but not fancy," I said.

"Well, of course it must be nice!" the clerk gushed. "We don't get married every day, do we?"

"Not an actual wedding dress," I told her, dutifully following Peter's instructions.

And then I added, "But I'd like white."

The minute I said it, I was sorry. It would be hard enough to find a suitable dress in my size. Limiting the color was folly.

"I mean, it doesn't actually have to be white," I stammered. "It can be any color. Well, not black, unless, I guess, if black's all you've got."

Lips pursed, brow furrowed, carefully examining me up and down, the salesclerk wasn't listening. "You know," she said, "I just might have something."

She led me to a fitting room and reappeared a few moments later with an elegant ivory dress. It hit just below the knee and was exquisitely tailored, with wide sleeves and a bateau neckline. I'd never seen a dress like that. The price was scary, but the zipper closed smoothly, and the fabric draped softly. I looked in the mirror and saw a bride.

Three days before we were to be married, on the day Peter and I had planned to tell our families, forecasters predicted a big storm for our wedding day. In a long phone call with the rabbi, we decided we had to move the wedding up to the very next afternoon. Most of our short guest list lived in town, and my dad could drive up from New Jersey. My mother and Craig, though, would have to catch a plane from Indiana right away. We hung up so I could call them, and Peter went to tell his parents our news.

"Hi, Mom!" I said. "Guess what! Peter and I are getting married!"

"Wonderful! Did he give you a ring?"

"Not yet."

"Oh," she said, with a thud of disappointment. "Then you're not really engaged."

"Maybe not," I said. "But our wedding's tomorrow."

We'd actually expected our families to react with unfiltered joy when we told them our news at the last minute, as though any plans they might need to break were irrelevant, as though any enjoyment they might have had in the run-up to the wedding wasn't their due. As though we didn't care whether they came or not.

My mother was furious, yelling at me and simultaneously hollering instructions over her shoulder to my brother. I cut her off. "Mom, listen, we have to hang up. I have to make another call, and you have to get plane tickets."

I called my father, who said he'd drive up the next morning and otherwise didn't comment.

Though my parents had been divorced for eleven years, they still couldn't be in a room together without creating a scene. After much deliberation, Peter and I had invited my mother to the ceremony and my father to the dinner afterward.

It sounds harsh, but it was the best we could think of, short of leaving one of them out altogether. As for the two of them, they took the enforced separation as a given, and both seemed to think they'd won in the deal.

As soon as I put down the phone, Peter's parents called to say they loved me and were thrilled I'd be joining their family.

Then his mother added, "Peter says it's not a fancy event and I shouldn't go get a manicure."

It was only the morning of the day before, plenty of time for a manicure, but he'd told her not to get one. He'd told her not to, and she was obeying, and I gave that no thought. I had a cake to bake.

My grandmother Julia made this cake for only the most important occasions. Though many had asked for the recipe, she'd kept it in the family with genteel evasion.

"Ten eggs, sometimes twelve, some flour, some sugar. The usual," she'd say. "I do it by feel."

My mother had the recipe and was equally protective of it, though less artful. If someone asked for it, she'd write it out on an index card with one or two ingredients slightly altered so it didn't quite measure up.

I had the recipe too, the real one, but I'd never made it. Now, alone in my Boston apartment, I took a carton of eggs out of the refrigerator and talked out loud to my grandmother, who was back in Indiana.

"I'm getting married tomorrow, Grandma," I said to the empty kitchen. "I'm sorry I couldn't invite you. Peter's kind of shy and needs the wedding to be really small," which is how I'd come to explain it to myself.

I pulled out the mixing bowls, the sifter, the measuring cups and spoons.

"I'm making your cake. For my wedding cake. And I'm using twelve eggs."

I spent much of that morning baking, and soon images of everyone eating the beautiful yellow and white marbled slices the following day merged with my memories of eating those same slices with my relatives at my grandmother's table over the years. It made me feel that my whole family, living and gone, was there with me, blessing my marriage.

My mother and Craig managed to get on one of the last flights to Boston that evening and arrived in snow that was not yet serious. In the morning, my father called to say he couldn't get down off his New Jersey mountaintop, snow already falling hard there and over a foot deep on his long, steep driveway.

"Well, that worked out," said my mother. "Now I can go to the dinner."

In the end, there were thirteen of us. Peter and I went in his station wagon, with the cake in a box on the floor of the back seat for safety. The heavy snow had finally hit Boston, and driving was rough. When we got to the synagogue, we found a message from the rabbi saying that he had to be in Israel a few days later and was leaving early, while planes were still flying. He'd arranged for a colleague to marry us.

Outside the synagogue windows, the snowfall was practically opaque when in stomped the substitute rabbi, a little guy in big boots.

"Who's the bride?" he demanded. "Stand over here. Who's the groom? Stand there. C'mon, c'mon, we have to get out of here!"

Throughout the service he tapped his foot and muttered, "Faster. C'mon."

At the ritual smashing of the wine glass, everyone yelled "Mazel tov!" and crowded around us in a tight knot. Suddenly the rabbi broke through. He'd grabbed my cake off its platter and was holding it against his chest with one hand and ripping off hunks with the other.

"Eat!" he commanded. "We have to get out of here! C'mon! C'mon!"

Some just stared at the wads he shoved in their hands. Others obediently took bites. Then he said abruptly, "I'm leaving, and you should too," and he ran.

Craig reminded me recently that despite the snow, we all made it to the restaurant. He says it was a good time. I couldn't say. My foremost memory from that day is the mauling of my cake, the image of it smashed against the rabbi's chest, crumbs tumbling down his jacket onto his pants, rolling into the cuffs; his fingers clawing off pieces, pressing them on people, throwing them at people, chunks dropping to the floor. I was in shock, frozen and unable to look away. Every piece ripped from that cake felt like part of my life being torn from me.

— 4 —

JEWELS IN THE SKY

PETER HAD HINTED THAT OUR honeymoon would be in Hawaii and that I should pack for warm weather. Not until after he'd checked our bags did he reveal that we were going to the Amazon rainforest, which back then we called the Amazon jungle. It was the only way he could have gotten me there. I was intimidated by travel, inept with foreign languages, and unnerved by poorly marked roads.

My mother had no sense of direction. To get to a local mall from her house, all she had to do was drive to the end of her street, turn right, and there it was. Still, each time she went there she set out as though in uncharted territory, unsure even which way to turn at the end of her driveway. The drive to my grandmother Julia's house so challenged her that she required silence in the car and had to lie down when we got there; I'd learned early that even a ninety-minute trip, mostly on one straight road, is daunting.

Except for the major cities, Brazil was a mystery to most travel agents in those days. Peter intended to find his own way around the Amazon, and he'd contacted two women with a small agency who booked Rio and Brasília for us, waiving their fees in exchange for his promise to bring back material they could use to put together jungle tours.

Sightseeing in the Amazon was rare and reckless, just up Peter's alley but not mine. He'd kept our trip a secret from our families as well as from me, and I couldn't stop thinking that if we didn't return, no one back home would know even what continent to search. What am I doing here? I asked myself, and the answer came immediately: Peter wanted to come.

We landed in Rio de Janeiro in the middle of Carnival. Thousands swarmed in from all over the globe, and the minute they hit the city, they stopped walking and started dancing. Streets, sidewalks, and even rooftops were packed solidly with dancers using any inch of space they could find to twitch their hips. Street bands, sometimes no more than ten feet apart, blared competing sambas at each other, and the grating racket of tin vuvuzelas came from all directions. We found we couldn't weave our way through the huge crush of people unless we joined one of the spontaneous conga lines, some several blocks long, that ignored stop lights and snaked their way through the crowds with the sheer energy of their size.

In vain, Peter had mapped out the bus routes that would get us where he wanted to go. Buses were useless. Unable to advance through the crowds in the streets, they were stuck, immobile, in the middle of it all, bouncing on their springs and rocking side to side as passengers, apparently unconcerned that they weren't getting anywhere, sang, blew horns and beat drums while they danced in the aisles, leaped on and off seats, and swung from the poles, sometimes by their knees.

Self-consciously at first, and then with abandon I'd never known, I swung my plus-size hips up and down the bus aisles with the rest of them, while Peter sat stolidly in his seat, arms crossed, face stony.

When we got to Brasília, things were very different. What would one day become green plazas were still barren wastelands between widely separated groupings of austere apartment buildings. Churches and schools were situated at mandated intervals, and residents got apartment assignments based on their professions. Peter loved the orderliness of it all, but I found the social engineering sinister. I felt watched, even in our hotel room. At the same time, I was amazed by all the different ways of living I was seeing and did not wish myself back in Boston.

Peter held our itinerary close to his chest, and I rarely knew our next destination until we arrived there. Manaus, on the river's edge, was a little town carved from the rainforest and constantly threatened by the resurgence of the undergrowth. Today, tourists swarm Manaus, a rainforest settlement turned fort turned town turned big city with an international airport. When we went there, it was a gathering place for rubber traders, with one small plane in and out each week.

A genius at ferreting out what to see and how to see it, Peter rented a little chugger of a car and drove us out along the main road until there was only rainforest as far as we could see in any direction. At a spot that to me looked no different from any other, he pulled over to the edge of the road and led me on foot through an invisible break in the dense vegetation. Just a few feet ahead of us was a narrow path topped with slats of wood, a tiny boardwalk a few inches above the ground. Walking behind Peter—the undergrowth reaching for us from the sides and up through the slats, the jungle getting wetter, darker, and heavier with each step we took—I looked back from time to time to make sure the otherworldly walkway wasn't vanishing behind us.

After about half an hour, the slats stopped abruptly in front of us, and a waist-high railing kept us from going any farther. Just ahead, the rainforest was impenetrable: ferns bigger than giants, vines the diameter of trees. The canopy, a hundred feet above, was so dense that even the sun could barely penetrate. We'd followed a mysterious wooden pathway into a prehistoric world.

Suddenly a brilliant flicker of cobalt blue burst high above us and was instantly gone. In the next moment there was a flash of neon yellow, gone just as quickly, then flashes of red, of green, of gold, of scarlet. Tropical birds were flying between branches high up in the canopy, their incandescent chest feathers exposed for just an instant when they crossed the odd crack of light breaking through the tree cover. We were in another world, where people were rendered the size of crickets, and a night-dark sky twinkled with emeralds, garnets, and sapphires. I was exploding with love for it all and for the husband who'd taken me there.

Peter had gotten us tickets on a riverboat with twelve other passengers and a single deckhand, none of whom spoke English. The Amazon River was the color of melted pennies and so wide that for long stretches we couldn't see either bank. It was like being in the middle of an ocean in a world with a different palette. After a while we could see lush bayous, where thick stands of reeds five feet tall or so cut the coppery water into fingerlike channels. The engines went silent, and the other passengers moved purposefully toward a small gate in the railing that ran around the edge of the deck. Clearly, I was the only person who didn't know what was happening.

Peter was beaming. "You'll never forget this," he said.

A few canoes emerged from the bayous and came alongside the riverboat. Wiry and almost naked, a lone man stood upright in each, piloting with a long pole. The deckhand on the riverboat unlocked the little gate, and the other passengers started clambering down the side of the boat on a wildly swaying ladder. In twos and threes, they gamely descended and took little leaps into the rocking canoes that pulled up one after another to collect them and carry them off into the bayous.

I refused to go. I wasn't light, wasn't agile, couldn't and wouldn't leap into a canoe. The waters hid crocodile-like caimans and schools of piraña. Those naked men and their puny poles would be useless in an attack. All the other canoes had left, but I didn't care. I wouldn't go.

The deckhand was furious. He put both hands on my back and pushed me to the ladder. Peter, already several rungs down, grabbed for my feet and tugged at them. By the time I was in the canoe, I was hysterical. The red water of the Amazon was only a couple of inches below the top of our canoe. When the riverboat left, we rolled madly in its wake; water sloshed in and soaked our shoes. I was terrified, sobbing loudly. Our navigator stood tall on the seat in front of me, impassively gazing toward shore. On the seat behind me, Peter wildly waved his arms, making the canoe rock even more.

"Stop being such a baby!" he kept saying. "Don't you understand? We're going to see the Victoria Regias!" Then he added, "Anyway, it's not a big deal if we tip over. Pirañas only go after injured prey. To be in danger, you'd have to be bleeding."

This wasn't true, but it was mean. He knew I had my period.

Silent, timeless, neither perturbed by the roils of history nor worried about what the future might bring, the magisterial Victoria Regia water lilies, nine feet across, floated serenely on the waters I so feared. To these noble lily pads, the distress of a woman in a canoe was imperceptible. I absorbed their calm and was composed.

-5-

COOKIES BY MY FACE

WHEN I TOLD OUR FAMILIES where we'd gone, his was impressed but not surprised. "That Peter!" they laughed. "How does he come up with these things?"

What my mother said was, "That's handy."

Back in Indiana after the wedding, she'd been unwilling to tell her friends she didn't know where we'd gone on our honeymoon. Getting it right entirely by accident, she'd told everyone we were in South America.

"What were you planning to tell them if we'd gone somewhere else?" I was fuming.

"I don't know," she answered. The phone amplified the slow draw on her cigarette and the blow of her exhalation. "I guess it would depend on where you'd gone."

On our first day back at Dearborn, Peter and I went in very early, slipped a wedding announcement under the principal's locked door, and went from room to room putting one on every teacher's chair. Then we waited in my classroom while the rest of the faculty showed up to start the day. Soon we heard shrieks of our own news echoing in the hallway as our colleagues gathered each other up and ran in to congratulate us.

Even with all the commotion, the questions, hugs, and wisecracks, I noticed a friend of mine was missing. She and I had started teaching at Dearborn at the same time, and we'd quickly become close. I hated keeping my engagement a secret from her and told myself that after Peter and I were married, she'd see the fun in what was essentially an elopement. But things hadn't played out so smoothly. A few months into the school year, she'd asked me, "What do you think about Peter, the science teacher? Something about him makes me nervous."

At that moment, I had the opportunity to open myself to the priceless intimacy of a good friend. I could have talked to her about what I was planning to do and perhaps seen it through clearer eyes than my own, but instead of taking seriously what she had to say, I simply said I hadn't noticed anything odd about him and changed the subject.

Finally, this friend came to my classroom, the wedding announcement still in her hand. She stayed by the door until she caught my eye, and then, with a look of disillusion and pity, she turned and walked out. We never spoke again.

The teachers threw us a party and gave us a blender, the year's hot gift. On the way home, Peter and I were still feeling celebratory—until we rounded a curve and saw fire engines and the remains of an emergency outside our building. The danger was over, the fire out. While the firemen packed up their gear, some children in pajamas were having a grand time stamping their feet in the puddles on the sidewalk while their parents stood around in small clusters and chatted.

An electrical fire in the apartment below ours had been doused quickly, but not before ours suffered significant smoke and water damage. A fireman grabbed a work light and escorted us up the pitch-black stairs to retrieve some of our things, but there was little to gather up. Everything was charred, soaked, or blackened by smoke. As his work light swept the bedroom, I saw that the closet door was scorched and ajar. On the floor lay my beautiful ivory wedding dress, soaked, streaked with oily smoke stains, and bearing right on the front, at the neckline, the big, black imprint of a fireman's wet and sooty boot.

Peter, our blender, and I stayed with his parents until we found a furnished one-bedroom apartment, and I set about toting up the losses. At the time of the fire, most of Peter's things were still back at his parents' house, but I'd lived in our apartment since right after Brandeis. The fire had taken my furniture, clothes, books, letters, photos—almost everything I owned.

"Come," said my mother-in-law, Blanche. "You need to shop."

Her credit card was in her hand even before we walked through the doors of the venerable Boston landmark, the Jordan Marsh department store, and started gathering things up. Blanket, broom, pillows, pots, lamp, light bulbs, washcloths, dish cloths. The receipt was as long as her arm.

"What else?" she asked. "Keep going."

When I was growing up, *Queen for a Day* was a popular game show borne of the mass-marketing opportunities to be mined from the real hardships of real people. Every week, women, always women, described their tragedies to a studio audience that selected, via a clap-o-meter, the contestant whose lot in life was worse than that of all the others. To the somber tones of *Pomp and Circumstance,* each week's queen—crowned in gold, robed in red, and usually sobbing uncontrollably— might receive, yes, that wheelchair her husband needed in order to work, but also a washing machine, a bra and girdle ensemble, a broiler pan, and a Formica dinette set, all donated by the show's sponsors. The sponsors' largesse was rewarded handsomely, as full-blown commercials of their products became the primary content of the show, interrupted briefly by flashes of the overcome queen. The queen no doubt was truly overcome, but she also knew to clutch her heart and practically faint with gratitude at each new prize, whether or not she wore girdles or liked to broil. Meanwhile, the losers were quickly escorted off camera with consolation prizes and the clear message that their critically ill child or impending homelessness was not sufficiently heart-wrenching. Gradually, I'd come to see something very wrong in the gladiatorial entertainment of pitting one terrible situation against another, and I'd stopped watching.

My own coronation, however, I thought was splendid. Blanche had intended to throw a reception in honor of our marriage, but after our fire, she diverted her party budget to this shopping spree. Never had my needs received so much attention. Whatever I needed was mine to take. Dishes, glasses, mirror, plunger, scissors, hangers, planters, pliers—I'll take that! And those! And two of those! Blanche didn't question my choices or comment on the cost. Robed in her largesse and with just the simplest, purest, most uncomplicated and adoring gratitude, I was Queen for a Day with a wedding reception's worth of treasure.

Actually, a dime-a-dozen product of the times is what I was. Whether genuinely or because I was supposed to, I reveled in being married and flaunted my wifehood at every opportunity.

I groaned to my colleagues about the red tape of changing my name. "Such a nuisance, but it has to be done."

I inserted "my husband" into any conversation I could. "Can I return this if my husband doesn't like it?"

One night I made a meatloaf in the shape of a heart.

But none of this was why I was the perfect wife for Peter. Rather, it was that I was so easily stifled. In his calculus, anyone who disagreed with him was against him, and that could mean me as readily as any stranger. On things as small as what to have for dinner or as large as whether to buy a car, I was always the one who gave in.

Only a few days after we got back from our honeymoon, Peter announced he was having a second phone put in. The new phone would have a separate number, and I was never to answer it. Many homes still had party lines then, and payphones were commonplace on the sidewalks. The thought of two separate phone lines in one household was preposterous, and the thought that a phone would be off limits to me in my own home was humiliating. I stood up to him for the first time.

"My friends want to talk to me, not you," he said.

"I'll tell them you're out. I'll take a message. That's what people do!"

We fought over that phone for two days before I put my foot down. Under no circumstances would we have a second phone.

A few weeks later I got home to discover that it had been installed and he'd invited several of his friends to dinner. With me right there, he gave them the new number and told them I wouldn't be answering it. Some of them shot odd looks at me, while I smiled and tried to look nonchalant. Even more mortifying were all the times he was out and I stood there, alone in the apartment, listening to it ring and not answering.

That phone was one of the things lost in the fire. The apartment we moved to afterward was in a neighborhood where the phone company was still converting party lines to private lines, and they wouldn't accept his order for a second number. Though I'd lived with that hateful phone only a few weeks, the affront of it stirred in me a thought still so primitive, I couldn't articulate it. It was something to do with being strong, but that was as far as I could take it.

One evening, I watched a woman on TV weep in front of her fire-destroyed house, and I thought, She's thin. She'll be fine. Her image stayed with me, and eventually I concluded that being strong was synonymous being thin.

I'd learned early on that there were people in this world who felt a calling to watch everything I ate. They took note, intoned food facts, and were almost energized by my diet failures. Both my parents were in this category. On a crowded downtown sidewalk, my father once yelled at me, "For crying out loud, you're jiggling!"

One winter break, when I was still at Brandeis, I arrived at his house for a visit and found he'd invited over his friend Antonio, who claimed to be a diet doctor. Antonio was skeletal as a stick figure. His wife was huge and welcoming, in the manner of an overstuffed chair. He'd once put her on a diet of nothing but black coffee and water all day and one Snickers at night.

That night, though, Antonio wasn't dealing in candy bars. I'd later learn he'd been instructed by my dad to take me in hand. When we all rose to go to the dining room, Antonio suddenly stood before me, arms on the doorjambs to block my way. With his bony face so close I could feel his breath on my eyes, he hissed, "Eat nothing. Do you hear me? Nothing." Then he turned and strode to the table.

No one acknowledged this had happened or even looked at me during the whole meal. Seven festive people clinked, drank, ate, and refilled, while I, the eighth, sat cowed in my place and ate nothing.

Back in high school, at my job in Ed Simon's lab, I'd spent the whole summer before my senior year tending to the fruit flies on autopilot and devoting my brainpower to concocting nutty schemes to avoid the first day of school. Jefferson High had a tradition of "class cords"—corduroy pants for the boys and narrow skirts for the girls. Freshmen's were kelly green, and sophomores' were red. Juniors wore an improbable red and black, and at last came senior yellow, the status symbol second only to a car. Seniors strutted in their yellows like aristocracy. Every August, those cords filled the stores, but there were none in my size. On the first day of school, every senior, every single one except me, would be wearing them.

"Well, what did you expect?" said my mother.

Three weeks before the start of school, my grandmother Julia came to visit. She immediately sized up the situation, tracked down the right yellow corduroy at a fabric store, and had a dressmaker make me a skirt that perfectly matched the ready-mades. Wearing it, I felt giddily like all the other girls, not seeing the reality of a size twenty ass in tight bright yellow.

My mother, however, saw disgrace. Slim and shapely, she was a knockout, a beauty who lived on coffee and cigarettes, and it made her crazy that I wasn't a prom-queen daughter. When Mom looked in the mirror, she saw the fairest in the land. If the meter reader rang the bell before her makeup was on, she wouldn't answer the door. Her couch cushions, her shower curtain rings, everything of hers, and that included me, had to impress her friends.

"I know you're gaining weight to spite me!" she'd scream, while to her bridge buddies she'd say, "I just don't know what to do about Marsha. I wish she'd eat less, but she says my cooking is too good."

My path to that custom-made skirt was littered with scores of failed diets and hundreds of fantasies of simply waking up thin one morning. Those fantasies were my preoccupation. Diets were my mother's. She tore crazy-making articles from *Woman's Day* and *Family Circle* and left them on my pillow. One said eat vegetables; another said eat protein. One said three meals a day; another said six small ones. The buttermilk diet, the Special K diet, the grapefruit diet—when my mother came home with eccentric assortments of groceries, I knew I was in for it.

One evening, I went to the dinner table and found only an empty glass and a can of vanilla Metrecal at my place. This was my introduction to the Metrecal Diet, a craze that in the early 1960s swept the country like lava lamps. Real food was outlawed and replaced with four cans a day of thick, chalky liquid, 225 calories each, for a total of 900 calories. I hated it, and I especially hated drinking it in the cafeteria, where my friends ate spaghetti and wisecracked about my liquid lunch.

Metrecal claimed their regimen would take off around three pounds a week, which I calculated condemned me to a six-month sentence. To speed things up, I decided to drink only two cans a day instead of four. Because my mother would never allow me to deviate like that from the plan, I hid the extra cans in the pockets of the winter coats hanging in the storage closet where we kept the out-of-season clothes.

On my third day of only 450 calories, I was so ravenous that I stopped at a bakery on my way home from school, bought two éclairs, and ate them both before I reached the next corner. At dinner that night, without a word, I pushed away the empty glass, got myself a plate, and served myself the potato-chip-topped tuna casserole. My mother screamed, "I hope you have a daughter just like you, so you know what you put me through!" and took to her room.

I wouldn't drink even one more can of Metrecal, but in the flush of my triumph, I forgot about the ones I'd hidden. Of course, my mother discovered them when winter came. When she confronted me, I insisted I had no idea how they got there, and I stuck to my absurd story. It was a hollow victory. I was still fat. Though my mother didn't believe me, I desperately wanted to get thin, and yet again, I'd failed.

I couldn't win. I never lost. I only gained.

Perhaps I emitted a pheromone that attracted people who wanted to be indispensable—the dinner hosts who announced, "There's no sugar in these," when I hadn't asked; the uncles who greeted me with, "You've put on weight"; the friends who incessantly asked, "How's the diet going?"

How was the diet going? I'd entered Brandeis at 200 pounds and emerged at 235, that's how.

One morning not long after our apartment burned, Peter went out early and I slept in. When I awoke in that little furnished apartment, I was hyper-aware of a new thought: that I needed to lose weight and that I'd better get on with it. There'd been no final straw, no health scare or split seam. Just the clear understanding that this was on me.

I knew I couldn't handle another public diet failure. I also knew that Peter, who ate large, would push food on me if I cut back and that, ultimately, I'd cave. I saw only one possibility. Resolute, I got out of bed and started a secret diet, hiding it from everyone, especially my husband.

It turned out to be surprisingly easy to hide a diet. In the beginning, I spread food around my plate to camouflage my leftovers, but it didn't take me long to discover that normal people regularly left food over and that camouflaging wasn't necessary. In my years of see-a-pretzel-eat-a-pretzel, I hadn't noticed.

Now, when colleagues brought cookies to work, I knew that if I didn't take one, somebody would inevitably ask, "Watching your waistline?" So I'd grab a large one, break it in half, put one piece down on my napkin, and hold the other piece up near my face when I spoke. No one realized it never reached my mouth. For the first time, I started losing weight, and I was certain it was because of the secrecy.

I avoided getting together with people I hadn't seen in a while, who would notice my weight loss as clearly as if it were time-lapse photography. I skipped a dinner with Brandeis friends by inventing a houseguest. Pretending to be sick, I sent Peter alone to his cousin's graduation. If someone commented that I looked thinner, I usually got away with, "I wish!" or, "Oh, you know me. I'm always going up and down."

I was about forty pounds down when a group of construction workers sitting on the sidewalk with open lunchboxes on their laps whistled and catcalled as I walked past, an iconic indignity that women suffer all the time. For me, it was the first time, and I'm ashamed to admit I loved it. I might have smiled at them. I think I swung my hips a little.

In a stunning example of both discriminating against women and forcing them to self-incriminate, the Boston school system required teachers to notify their principals and leave their jobs as soon as they realized they were pregnant. I knew there were women who held off confessing as long as they could get away with it, and I understood their anxiety. Like them, I feared "showing."

Instead of buying clothes in smaller sizes, I wore my big ones and used bulky sweaters to cover up how loose they were.

At restaurants with Peter, I'd go on and on about how good the food was, then groan that I was too full and slide some from my plate to his. As my weight kept dropping, my obsession with secrecy turned into a bona fide belief in magic. I was actually convinced that if anyone discovered I was dieting, the spell would break and the pounds rush back in and reinflate me.

About halfway through my weight loss I was still hiding in my large clothes, but I really needed new bras. Always before, bra shopping had been a quick affair. A clerk would glance at me and go dig out from the back the one or two styles that might fit. In a black dress with epaulets, her silver hair ruthlessly teased, the clerk I drew on this particular day hurled questions at me. "Separation? Wonder Bra? Cone?" What *was* all this? On commission and exasperated by my hesitation, she started looking past me for a more promising customer.

"I've lost some weight," I said. "I'm not sure what I need."

Focusing on me again, she eyed my bust with a self-assured squint, told me to follow her, and marched toward the fitting rooms, snatching bras off racks as she went.

"Those seem a little big," I ventured, as she hung her choices on a hook. I'd already taken off my sweater, and she turned to look at my now-naked chest. In her initial appraisal, she hadn't picked up that my downsized breasts were puddled at the bottom of ridiculously oversized cups. With a raised eyebrow that I took as a begrudging salute, she swept up the ones she'd just brought and a few minutes later returned with new ones.

Of course, bulky sweaters wouldn't work forever. At about three sizes down, I walked into the teachers' lounge one lunchtime and Brenda, a fourth-grade teacher and avid collector of other people's dramas, jumped up from her seat at the head of the table, pointed both hands at me like pistols, and shrieked, "You've lost a ton!"

Everyone swiveled to look at me. The room filled with "You look terrific!" and "How did we miss it?!" Feeling the loss of the room's attention, Brenda called out above the noise, "Want to know how I knew? You could always hear her thighs rubbing together when she came down the hall. Today there was no noise!"

For just an instant I held my breath—literally, crazily expecting my lost pounds to surge back in. Then I was laughing out loud at my own foolishness and walking tall into a circle of women who were happy for me and admired what I'd accomplished. It hadn't been magic. It had been me.

In all, I lost six sizes, four that year and two the next. For a long time, whenever people raved about my transformation, Peter would smack his forehead and grin like a doofus.

"Can you believe it? I didn't even notice! I'm such an idiot!"

It humiliated me—for myself, for him, for us—but I couldn't get him to stop. His mother, not at all amused by his performance, pulled me into a corner one day and whispered, "How could he not notice? Doesn't he sleep with you?" I shrugged her off, not ready to think about my marriage.

At about that time, I noticed I was finding it hard to get a handle on my new size. It started with an elevator. When the doors opened for me, there were already several people inside. I went to step in, and suddenly I wasn't sure I would fit. Embarrassed, I mumbled some excuse and took the stairs.

After a while, I couldn't tell how my body compared to, say, yours, or whether I would fit into the back seat of someone's

Beetle easily or not at all. There were times, sometimes two or three in the same week, when my own reflection startled me by being either much smaller or much larger than I expected. One time I appeared so unrealistically thin in a store window, I put my bags on the sidewalk and stood there comparing each passerby to their reflection, trying to assess the extent of the window's distortion. There wasn't any.

It wasn't that I had the *wrong* notion of my size. It was that I had *no* notion. Every time I saw myself in a mirror could have been the first time. I wasn't at all alarmed, just intrigued. I figured my eyes or brain simply had to adjust after years of seeing a different person in the mirror, and I was game to just live with it. Sometimes, though, I got nervous and worried that I was kidding myself. Maybe the weight loss hadn't made as big a difference as I thought.

Particularly if a large woman walked by, I'd ask Peter, "Am I thinner than her?" He couldn't stand it. Charging two or three steps ahead of me to make his point, he'd call back over his shoulder, "Stop fishing for compliments!" I soon stopped asking, and over time the episodes became fewer and farther between. The last one would occur in a restaurant about twenty years later, when someone would tell me I was slim, and I would finally see it.

– 6 –

ODYSSEY

I'D JUST STARTED MY SECRET DIET when Peter sprang on me that he wanted to live in Japan for two years. His enthusiasms always seemed to rise from nowhere and take him over. Usually I went along with them, but this was far bigger than a sudden compulsion to find Boston's best ice cream or fish chowder. I'd been teaching for less than a year and wanted to establish myself as a teacher. I'd also resigned myself to the fact that living with Peter meant living with bolts from the blue, and I didn't want to be seven thousand miles from home if something really crazy happened.

Arguing wouldn't work, so I said, "That might be fun someday," and was relieved when he didn't press the matter. A few days later, quietly, matter-of-factly, he said that with or without me, he was going to Japan. If I didn't go with him, we'd see each other when he came back on visits. He didn't know how long he'd stay there or how often he'd come back and would decide those things over time.

The shame of a wife abandoned seeped into me. I told him I'd go if he promised me two things. One, we'd stay for no more than two years, and two, we'd buy open-dated return tickets so no matter what befell us in Japan, we'd have our way home. He accepted my terms.

We decided to leave at the end of the summer following my second year of teaching. During our two remaining summers in Boston, Peter would run the camp science program he'd managed for several years, and I'd study Japanese in an intensive summer school course, nine hours a day for eight weeks.

The theory was that at least one of us should know some Japanese when we got there, but it was crazy that the role fell to me. After two years of high school German, all I remembered was *Guten Tag, Luisa* and *Wenigstens gibt es Reis*. At Brandeis, after Peter took me to *Don Giovanni*, I'd impulsively signed up for Italian, propelled by the illusion that I'd learn to read opera libretti in the original language. Beginning Italian was widely known as a gut course, so I cockily took it for a grade instead of pass/fail. My D knocked me off the Dean's List and convinced me I wasn't a language person.

Japanese completely confounded me. How could every noun be both plural and singular? How could there be different numbers for counting bound things, glassfuls, people, portions, flat things? And who could ever make sense of that sentence structure? The literal English translation of the Japanese for "I don't understand" was "As for me, understanding isn't." "How many pencils are there?" was "There are pencils to the extent of how many long, cylindrical units?"

"You're living my dream!" wrote Worth. "Learn the kanji so you can teach them to me when you get back." Kanji—those elegant, multi-stroke Chinese characters used in written Japanese. Except for toilet, subway, restaurant, book, person, and Japan, I never would learn them, which meant I wouldn't learn to read. For a long time, it looked as though I'd never learn to speak, either.

Then came the breakthrough. Just as in the water scene from the film *The Miracle Worker,* when the deaf and blind Helen Keller suddenly understands her teacher's finger spelling, suddenly I could form Japanese sentences. I could count things of every size and shape! I had no need of plural nouns! This marvelous language, developed on the other side of the world in isolation from Western languages, could say everything I would ever want to say, not only with a different vocabulary, but with an entirely different way of coming at a thought. In that watershed moment, I would have visited a kingdom on Mars just to see how their verbs worked.

Travel to Japan is so common now, the culture and cuisine so familiar, it's difficult to remember how unusual our plans were. When our friends and family heard we were moving to Japan, most bowed and said, "Ah so-o-o," and grinned at their own imagined originality. One couple predicted, "You'll eat a lot of Chun King," a canned chow mein that was questionably Chinese and made no pretense at all of being Japanese. Many in our parents' generation lectured us about Pearl Harbor. One guy told us to be sure to see Gilbert and Sullivan's *The Mikado* before we went, so we'd "know what we were getting into."

The exception was Grandma Minnie. She was enraptured by the notion that Peter and I were off to Japan. With a poet's sensibility, she invoked beautiful images of what we'd find there, images pulled from her remarkable memory of the hundreds of books she'd read. About our trip, she had no reservations and one request. "See it, smell it, taste it, touch it, feel it," she urged me, "and please, when you come back, I would love a pair of real Japanese slippers."

By the time Peter and I arrived in Tokyo, we'd worked hard to learn what to expect. Still, we would find the warmth of the Japanese people, the scenery, the pottery, lacquerware, fabrics, the music, dance, theater, cuisine, the cleanliness, the sense of personal safety, and the reverence for history not only beyond our expectations, but awe-inspiring.

In the winter before our departure, a Japanese friend and I went to the Boston Public Library and looked up English conversation schools in the Tokyo phone book. While she addressed envelopes in Japanese, I handwrote letters in English, inquiring about teaching opportunities for Peter and for myself. We mailed Peter's letter in half the envelopes and mine in the rest.

A couple of offers came quickly. By good fortune, mine was from Nichibei Kaiwa Gakuin, the Japanese Language Institute. It was the largest English language school in the country, but we didn't know that yet. In fact, we knew nothing about Nichibei and nothing about the school that had hired Peter. All we had were acceptance letters agreeing to our proposed September start date and confirming that the schools would sponsor our work visas.

My visa arrived well before our departure, along with a letter that said a Mr. Watanabe, from the Nichibei staff, would meet us at the airport, get us settled into a hotel, and accompany us as translator on our apartment search with a real estate agent they'd engaged for us.

We still hadn't gotten Peter's visa by the time we left Boston, but we weren't worried. We'd be spending a full month visiting friends and relatives on our way to the West Coast, and all our mail was being forwarded to Peter's parents. His mother would watch out for the visa as we made our way across the country and send it on to us. But by the time we'd made it all the way to a friend's home in Hawaii, it still hadn't come. We were trapped on Maui, running out of money, and wearing out our welcome with our host.

Three or four times a day, Japan time, we tried to reach Peter's school. That meant often calling through the night because of the nineteen-hour time difference. No one ever answered. Not knowing where else to turn, we contacted Nichibei. They put Mr. Watanabe on the case, and when he also couldn't get Peter's employer on the phone, he went to their address. The place was deserted and padlocked.

Nichibei got busy. They immediately issued Peter a student visa to study in their Japanese language program, and with both visas in hand, we boarded our international flight. After Peter fulfilled the requirements of the student visa, Nichibei issued him a work visa to teach in their English program, and once again the two of us were working at the same school.

On the ground floor of a two-story concrete building as forgettable as a budget motel, our apartment was a rectangle divided by sliding doors into two square rooms. Going in, we left our shoes in a tiny sunken entranceway, stepped up one step into a wood-floored room, and slid our feet into waiting slippers. Along one wall of this front room were a sink, a tiny counter-height refrigerator, and a two-burner stove. Across the room from the cooking area was a Western-style table the size of a bridge table, with two Western-style chairs. Usually, we dropped our bundles on that table and crossed through this utilitarian space straight to the heart of the apartment, the tatami room.

Tatami mats, traditional Japanese flooring made of dense rice straw covered with soft rush straw, are beautiful and remarkably strong. One never wears shoes or slippers on tatami, so we left our slippers on the wood-floor side of the sliding doors and stepped through in our socks.

Since tatami size is standard, the size of a room is often stated in mats. Ours was an eight-mat room, about twelve feet square. We sat on cushions on the tatami and ate, worked, read, and entertained at a wooden table about fourteen inches high in the room's center. At night we moved the table and floor cushions into a corner and spread out our futons, luxe Japanese mattresses, thick and comfortable, bearing no resemblance to the "futon" sleep sofas marketed in the US today. In the morning, we folded up the futons, put them away in a closet made for that purpose, and moved the table and cushions back to the center of the room. Before long, Peter and I were stepping in and out of footwear, sitting and sleeping on the floor, and washing before getting into a bathtub as naturally as if we'd never done anything else.

The bath was Japanese style, to us a true enlightenment of what bathing could be. We washed ourselves in a separate tiled area and only then, when we were clean and rinsed, climbed into the tub for a hot soak. Ours was square, big enough for one person sitting up, and deep enough for the water to cover the shoulders. Sometimes I'd soak for half an hour, constantly adding hot water and letting the hubbub of the day dissolve. Often, we went to the community baths, which were as deep as our bath at home but big enough for many people to soak at once. Conversation in the women's bath was friendly and quiet. Occasionally another Western woman would appear, but usually I was the only one, at first a curiosity to the other women but soon just another participant in the friendly chatter.

My first-year Japanese that had sounded so impressive in a Massachusetts classroom got me nowhere in Tokyo. I enrolled in one Japanese class after another, and, what with living in a Japanese neighborhood and loving the language, I learned to speak fluently.

I joined a chorus in which I was the only foreigner, and before long, I started taking private voice lessons with the choral director, a hammy vocal coach who mistook me for his ticket to international recognition. Soon he booked me to sing Handel arias in a recital he was putting together, and my search for a serious accompanist led me to Esther, a pianist from the McGill Conservatory. Mansion, maid, chauffeur, time on her hands—Esther was a corporate wife living in rich-expat style and eager to make music.

Her husband, Sol Mester, was CEO of Mattel Toys Southeast Asia, a Japanese-American joint venture. I first met him at a party in their home, where our entire apartment would have fit in one corner of the living room. The affair was like a champagne ad come to life. Dressed-up people stood around in little clusters, occasional bursts of laughter breaking through the buzz then blending again into the general hum. Strolling waitstaff refilled empty glasses and offered trays of sushi and tiny lamb chops.

At one point, Sol and I found ourselves alone in a corner, having a conversation that we both enjoyed: He loved talking about his work, and I loved hearing about it.

"So what actually is a joint venture?" I asked.

"In this case," he said, "partners from both Japan and America jointly own the company. We promote Mattel toys to the Japanese market. My board is half Japanese and half American."

I'd been in Japan more than a year by then and knew that schools, restaurants, stores, and even the post office and police department operated very differently from ours back home.

"That must be hard," I said. "The Japanese and Americans do things so differently."

"Sometimes it's tough," he said, and he described a recent board fight and how he'd intervened.

"Didn't that make the other side stop trusting you?" I asked.

"Absolutely," he said, and he told me how he'd dealt with that.

Whatever Sol said, I had another question. "Didn't they resent . . . ?" "Weren't you worried they'd . . . ?" "How did you get them to . . . ?" I was wholly caught up in Sol's world when Peter, tired of circulating on his own, and Esther, angry that Sol was ignoring their other guests, arrived together and pulled us from our corner.

Despite my original insistence on leaving after two years, I now wanted to stay on in Japan as much as Peter did. We agreed to a third year and decided not to wait until we were back in Boston to start a family. This meant we'd need a larger place. When we learned that two of our colleagues were leaving Tokyo and that their large apartment, legendary around Nichibei, was about to be available, we immediately contacted the landlady and arranged to meet with her the following day.

A traditional yellow earthen wall capped with clay tiles surrounded the property, and an intricate wrought-iron gate opened into a serene Japanese garden where white stone paths wound among painstakingly groomed maples, bamboo, azaleas, and camellias. A stone lantern, mantled with the moss of many years, provided gentle lighting near a small, ornate iron bench. Koi swam around a pond and nibbled at the algae growing on artfully placed rocks, one of which was a perfect sunning spot for three brass turtles. There was even a sozu, a kind of fountain made from a length of bamboo that fills from a spout above until, full and top-heavy, it tips over to empty into the pond, sounding a hollow clack against a rock before turning upright to fill again. A sozu was often found in meditative gardens and temples, so calming and somehow reassuring was its deep, resonant sound.

The garden wrapped around two sides of the house, once the home of a prosperous official. After his death, his widow lived there with her daughter and son-in-law, who died when she was ninety and her daughter around sixty. No longer needing such a large house, the two women had converted the second floor into a separate apartment by adding a kitchen, Japanese bath, and private entrance.

It had two tatami rooms, each more than double the size of the one in our current apartment, and the mats were edged in brocade, not the usual plain brown binding. The larger room had a classic tokonoma, an alcove for displaying treasured objects, and the landladies had hung there a hand-painted scroll depicting a mountainous landscape.

Hand-painted murals adorned the sliding doors that separated the tatami rooms, and above them was a wooden transom, elaborately hand-carved with branches and blossoms. More sliding doors, these with small panes of translucent white paper made from mulberry leaves, opened to reveal a wooden-floored enclosed balcony, called an engawa, that ran along two sides of the apartment, its large windows overlooking the garden.

It was a calm and quiet place, a world secluded from the streets just beyond the garden wall. Incredibly, the rent was hardly more than what we were already paying, and the two women were happy to have us. They'd had good luck with Nichibei teachers, and since neither of them knew English, they liked that I spoke Japanese.

A few months later I was ecstatic to discover I was pregnant, but Peter's behavior worried me. He could be calmly sitting and talking to someone, nothing amiss, and suddenly start talking too loudly, almost hollering, or crossing one leg over the other and shaking his foot so hard his knee jerked up and down with it. At one Nichibei faculty meeting, he leaned forward almost double in his chair and began running his knuckles back and forth across his lips, as though feverishly playing a harmonica, oblivious to the teachers' nudging each other to take a look. For the first time, I saw him through the eyes of others. Embarrassed for him and for myself, I kept my eyes locked on the meeting handouts.

The reassuring clack of the sozu and the garden wall that muffled the noise of the outside world became precious to me as I worked to suppress my fears that something could be seriously wrong with my husband.

Japan was a glorious place to have a baby. I'd had no idea about the deep love of babies in Japanese culture and the consideration for pregnant and postpartum women. It was easy to find a doctor and hospital that allowed fathers in the delivery room and would let me nurse the baby immediately after birth, things that would still be hard to find in Boston years later.

I loved being home with our new daughter, Ellen, and when my maternity leave was over, I cut my Nichibei hours to the minimum required to maintain my visa. We put a rocking chair out on the engawa, where I often sat and nursed her. Every day I'd strap her on my back, Japanese style, and go on my daily rounds to the neighborhood shops. Sometimes I didn't even need anything, but I couldn't get enough of the way the shopkeepers and customers flocked around her. She was quite the sensation, with her round Western eyes, and people constantly came up, covered their own eyes with their hands, and played Japanese peekaboo with her. "*Inai inai ina-a-ai . . . BA!*"

One weekend when Ellen was about eight weeks old, Peter took her out for a walk. It was his first time alone with her. On their way back to the apartment, she started fussing, and his attempts to settle her down only upset her more. By the time they got home, he was so frustrated he practically threw her at me. "You knew she'd cry! Why did you let me take her?" he shouted, and he started pulling drawers out of the dresser and hurling them to the floor.

Ellen started screaming. Anything I did to try to calm either of them only angered Peter more. He picked up a drawer from the floor and threw it a second time. His body and an obstacle course of wooden drawers blocked the only way out. Curling myself tightly around Ellen, I slowly stepped backwards into the adjoining tatami room and closed the sliding door between us and the mayhem. Frantically, I tried to quiet her, but with the din of drawers crashing on drawers, it was impossible.

Abruptly, the crashing stopped. I heard Peter run down the stairs and out of the apartment, but, afraid that he might return, I stayed where I was for quite some time, trying to calm myself and my baby before I cautiously slid open the door to the other room. Empty drawers and everything that had been in them were strewn all over, the chaos of the disorder eerily out of place in the heavy quiet. I worked my way through the clutter to the rocking chair and sang quietly to Ellen until she relaxed and my own trembling stopped. As the shock wore off, I realized I was in exactly the situation I'd feared when Peter first brought up moving to Japan—far from home and hit by a dangerous bolt from the blue.

Were there systems in place here to protect my daughter and me? Should I go to the police? The American Consulate? Would anyone even believe me? There was no obvious victim. No one had been injured; the drawers had been thrown on the floor, not at Ellen or me. And if someone did believe me, then what? Peter's rage at being asked by officials to explain himself would be terrible. Even if I took Ellen and went back to Boston, I had nowhere to live and no way to support us. I was trapped.

When I finally got out of the rocker, cleaned up the mess, and put Ellen to bed, Peter still wasn't home. I went to bed, grateful for that, at least.

– 7 –

DISCOVERED BY SOL

WHEN I WOKE UP THE next morning, Peter was in the kitchen, acting as though nothing had happened. Afraid of another tirade, I did the same. He'd just left for Nichibei when the phone rang, a bit early for social propriety. It was Sol, the Mattel Toys executive. We hadn't spoken since the night of his and Esther's party, a year earlier, and he got right to the point.

"I want you to do some consulting for me."

"Sol," I said, "I think you've misunderstood something. I'm a teacher and a singer, not a consultant."

"Look, I've got a serious problem. I need someone I can trust, and I think you can handle the situation."

"I don't even know what a consultant does. I'm not a business person."

He ignored me. His Japanese and American board members had been deadlocked for days over a business matter, he said, to the point that now they wouldn't even go in the same room. Someone on the board had leaked the feud to the staff, and when Sol arrived at his office that morning, two men who said they spoke for about three hundred staff were waiting for him with an ultimatum—do what the Japanese directors wanted, or the three hundred would resign en masse. Questions ricocheted in my head. How had it come to this? Surely so many people wouldn't give up their jobs? Or, in Japan, would they?

I didn't need business savvy to realize that this was a big mess, and I was surprised at how much I was drawn to it. Still, Sol was asking me to do something I didn't know how to do. It made no sense. My one stint in a business had been a summer job in the office of a junkyard when I was sixteen. Surely Tokyo was teeming with real business consultants.

Sol and I went back and forth.

"I don't know anything about business."

"I think you can help me."

"You misunderstand."

"No, *you* misunderstand!" he said, with the peevish finality of someone used to getting his way. "You're a natural!"

And then he told me what he proposed to pay. I was stunned.

He waited.

I thought hard, swallowed, and gave him my answer. "Sol," I said, "I don't know how to do anything worth that much money."

He tried to talk but couldn't stop laughing. He gulped air, got control, then snorted and was laughing again, which got me laughing too.

"Look," he said, when we could finally speak. "That's not a lot of money for me. I can risk it. You get them back to the table, and I'll take it from there. Try it. If it doesn't work out, we'll end it. No harm done. How about a couple of afternoons a week?"

Now I was done arguing with him and was arguing with myself. My time with Ellen was so precious . . . but this was really tempting . . . but she was so little. . . .

The chance to be in this new stew and the availability of a wonderful babysitter won out. I still didn't understand what I'd be doing at Mattel, but if Sol thought I could handle it, why wouldn't I try? I started the following week.

Sol walked me around and introduced me as an American consultant temporarily working in Tokyo, emphasizing "American" because in Japan at that time, being an American outweighed the drawbacks of being a woman.

Murmuring, "Thanks for doing this," he left me with the employee representatives behind the mass resignation threat and retreated. From then on, I saw him only at the end of each workday, when I debriefed him and he gave me advice. A mentor, I would call him today, but that word wasn't broadly in use yet.

Fortunately, the company operated in English. I didn't know business jargon even in English, much less in Japanese, and in my chorus I'd learned the hard way that using freshly acquired vocabulary entailed some risk. We'd been working on a Benjamin Britten piece, and the director had had me take over a rehearsal to teach the pronunciation and phrasing of the English text. Galvanized by the baton in my hand, I'd confidently used words I'd picked up from him. A month went by before an alto shyly let me know that I'd called the basses something equivalent to "swain" and had used a sexual reference to tell them to prolong a particular vowel. In the moment, no one had let on.

It turned out that the Mattel employee reps knew almost nothing about the specific issue that had riven the board. At least they wouldn't try to engage me on the business merits. The fact that I'd been brought in, I told them, was surely a sign that management was responding to their concerns. "All my work will be focused on uniting the board," I said, "but that will take a little time. Why don't you relax your timeline and give me a chance to move things along?"

They weren't buying it. In another half hour I was to meet with the Japanese board members, and clearly there'd be no defusing the staff before then.

"I'll be happy to meet with you again next week," I said, "but if you take action between now and then, my work will be stopped."

They agreed to sit tight for a week. All I'd accomplished was a brief pause, and in the process I'd gone too far. I'd essentially agreed to keep working with them if they played nice, when what really had to happen was for them to step back. I didn't know how to turn this around, and my heart was beating fast. With thirty minutes until my next meeting, I stepped outside for some air.

Just around the corner from the Mattel building was a small neighborhood with the usual little shops lining the streets. The pickle shop, fruit and vegetable shop, meat shop, noodle shop, home goods shop . . . many had been run by the same families for generations, and curtained doorways in the backs of most led to rooms where two or three generations might live. On such a beautiful day, the second-floor windows were opened wide, with colorful futons draped over the sills to air. Housewives were going from shop to shop, some carrying the empty bowls that were a sure sign they were headed for the tofu shop. There, the proprietor would use a large paddle with a handle about five feet long to fish blocks of freshly made tofu from the bottom of a deep vat of water and put them in the provided bowls. Even after a quiet twenty-minute walk in this untroubled scene, I went back to Mattel no less apprehensive about my next meeting.

On the fourth floor of Mattel's no-frills concrete building, there wasn't a hint of the enticing weather or the cheerful colors of the neighborhood. The Japanese directors impeccably welcomed me, but it quickly became clear that unless I found a way to pull them along, we wouldn't get anywhere. When I asked about their concerns, I got answers like, "That's very complicated." After several more failed attempts to get them talking, one of the directors asked, "What will you report to the American directors?"

Of course. How naive I'd been. To these men, the American board members and I were of the same tribe. "I won't tell them anything you say," I answered, "and I won't tell you anything they say, either."

The air in the room lightened a little, and very tentatively we started to work. Still guarded, they offered up fragments of what had led to the board's breakdown, but none of what they said seemed consequential enough to have brought things to this pass. I let them go on for a few minutes before I interrupted.

"Thank you," I said. "Now let's talk about the situation with the staff."

Surprisingly, most of them said they knew nothing about the staff's ultimatum. I suspected at least one of the men sitting there had had a hand in it, but no one confessed, and I didn't push. Grumbles that the employees should never have been involved came from all around the table, and soon two men stood and walked toward the door, announcing they were on their way to speak to the employees' representatives. When Sol debriefed me at the end of the day, I was able to tell him that the Japanese directors had gotten the staff to stand down.

On the bus home, Mattel fell into the background, and I worried that things had not gone well with the sitter, that Peter was creating a scene at home, that Ellen was hysterical. I didn't know how I could face it. But Ellen was fine. Peter was calm. We had a quick dinner, and I went straight to bed. He and I still hadn't talked about the big incident of a few days earlier, and I was glad to avoid it for another day.

The minute I met the American directors, a few of the feistier ones launched into a harangue about how recklessly their Japanese counterparts were acting. At their first pause I broke in and asked, "What about the rest of you? Do you all agree?" The others seemed dubious but unwilling to disagree with their colleagues. When I asked what else might have brought the board to such a pass, I got answers that were no more substantive than what I'd gotten from the Japanese directors. Toward the end of the meeting, I asked what they thought it would take for the two sides to get together.

Japanese capitulation, it seemed.

"I don't think that's going to happen," I said, "and I'm guessing you won't capitulate either. We've got serious work ahead of us."

Twice a week for the next several weeks I shuttled back and forth between the two conference rooms where the directors caucused in separate, equally obstinate groups. Although of course there was no such thing, my mind has hung a Japanese flag outside one of those rooms and an American flag outside the other. Getting them to talk about resolving the stalemate was futile. One day, fed up, I sarcastically challenged a particularly truculent American to tell me how the board standoff was good for the company. He gave me flimflam, and the others looked down at their hands. Later, I asked the Japanese directors the same question, and they looked down too. Not long afterward they all seemed to tire of their war.

The directors agreed to meet together, and as I led both groups in a self-conscious parade to a bigger room, I felt jubilant and also disappointed. The success felt fabulous, except that these men were going on to serious matters, and I was going home.

Though not just yet, as it turned out. When we got to the large board room, the Japanese went to one side of the table, the Americans to the other, and they all looked at me with expressions I read as, "Okay, big shot. Now what?" All I could think of was to ask them to describe what would happen if they continued on like this. One brave speaker said, "It would be catastrophic."

"What do you mean by catastrophic?" I asked. "What would that look like? How would you know if a catastrophe was happening?"

After we compiled a sobering list, they all conceded for real that it was time to settle down and get to work. Someone went to get Sol, and my work was truly done. I'd been a consultant for nine weeks.

For years, I wondered why Sol had tapped me. Ultimately, I concluded that he felt things had gone too far for all of them, and that what they needed was a way to stand down without losing face. I'm guessing he felt I was bright enough to figure out the basics and thoughtful enough to avoid causing an explosion. He just needed me to do reasonable things to nudge people in the direction they already wanted to go in. By agreeing to consult for him, I'd suited his, the board's, and the staff's ambitions. Though at the time I didn't have ambitions of my own, later, when I did, it would turn out I'd suited those as well.

– 8 –

A DIFFERENT PERSON

LIFE WITH PETER WAS GETTING harder. He was quick to anger and slow to get over it. He imagined slights at Nichibei and insisted that colleagues who'd been friends were now enemies. When I stayed on good terms with them, he smoldered.

Once he happened into the same restaurant where one of those friends and I were having lunch. He came over to our table and conspicuously ignored her.

"I need a word with you," he said stiffly.

"Sure," I said. "What's up?" My composure was fake.

"I mean in private."

And he turned his back on me and walked over to the window, where he stood and waited.

"Looks like I'm in the doghouse," I said to my friend, rolling my eyes and flashing a conspiratorial smile, though the pit of my stomach was clenched. "I'll be right back."

"I told you . . ." Peter started, but I cut him off.

"She's my friend," I said quietly. "And I am having lunch with her. We can talk more about this at home, but not here. If you make a fuss, I won't be a part of it."

He stormed out onto the street, a tornado of a man.

"Men!" I said, back with my friend. "Can't live with 'em. Can't live without 'em."

But my hands were trembling on the table. She reached across and put hers on top of them.

I dallied at work at the end of the day to avoid facing warfare at home, but there wasn't any. When I walked in, he walked out.

He came back late. I was reading on my futon, and when I heard him coming up the stairs, I turned out the light and pretended to be asleep, my heart pounding.

The next day, Mr. Hasegawa, a senior manager at Nichibei, pulled me aside. "Your husband seems different," he said. "It doesn't feel right."

"I know," I said. "We're about to go on vacation. Hopefully a little rest will do him good."

Peter and I had fought about this vacation. He'd come home one day and simply announced that he'd made our plans for the upcoming semester break. We were going to Taiwan, he said. The itinerary was set and paid for. We'd start out in the countryside and end up in Taipei.

I wasn't the same person who'd given him carte blanche over our honeymoon. Not that he didn't plan good trips, but I worked hard, and free time was a luxury. I wanted a say in how to spend it.

"Then this is the last vacation we'll take," he said, and it was.

In the Taiwan countryside, getting out of our cab from the airport, I looked up at the towering mountains and cried out, "Peter, look! The mountains on our scroll! They're real!" Above me were distinctly conical mountains, complete with little rings of cloud around their sharply pointed tops. They looked exactly like the mountains I'd seen so often in Chinese art. I was amazed. I'd thought those images were stylized, but they were true to life.

Peter bloomed, as he always did with travel, and I was able to relax into the trip. By the time we were in Taipei, I thought we might be fine after all.

On the last day, we went to the stunning National Palace Museum, home to hundreds of thousands of Chinese imperial antiquities sent from the mainland to Taiwan by Chiang Kai-shek in the run-up to war. At lunch, our waiter took our order and, with much pantomime and a little English, asked if he could take Ellen into the kitchen to meet the chefs. We smiled and handed her over in her baby seat. Never would we have allowed this in America, but it happened so regularly in Japan, we were used to it and had even come to consider an occasional child-free break during a meal a perk of eating out.

When they hadn't brought her back after a longer time than usual, Peter said, "Maybe it's like that woman in China," and launched into the horrible old joke about an American woman who pantomimed to her Chinese waiter to take her little dog to the kitchen and give it some water. At the end of her meal, when she asked for her pet back, she learned she'd just enjoyed him in a stew.

We ran to the kitchen.

Two men were slicing cabbages and peppers from piles higher than their heads, while a third shuttled the trays of prepared vegetables to the stove and returned with empties to be refilled.

In another area, two men chopped meat with cleavers faster than our eyes could follow, their blades, in perfect rhythm, alternating in the same air space. There were pots of rice the size of washtubs, and bowls of chopped herbs waited in neat rows near the soup pots for one broth or another to be ladled in. Waiters came through the in-door from the dining room and called out new orders as it swung closed behind them. Others made for the out-door, balancing dishes up the lengths of both their arms.

In the center of it all, on a stainless-steel counter, sat Ellen. She was in her little seat, holding a wooden rice paddle like a scepter. One of the staff watched over her, singing a children's song in Chinese and making hysterically funny faces, while three others flanked him and pantomimed riotous laughing at his antics. The waiters gaily called out "Hello baby!" and "Bye-bye baby!" each time they came or went through the swinging doors. She laughed at the singer's goofiness and graced the waiters with grins. One of the cooks tried his English on us.

"She is a most delicious," he said.

With smiles all around, we scooped up our daughter and headed back to our table to finish eating. As soon as we left the kitchen, Peter said, "How could you have allowed them to take her?"

"Everything's fine," I said, adjusting Ellen's sweater. "And we both said okay. We've said okay hundreds of times."

"Don't you ever criticize me in front of her again," he said, his voice deep, low, a new fight voice more ominous than the old.

When we got back to Tokyo, there was a message at Nichibei for me to call one of the directors I'd worked with at Mattel.

He was an executive at a fast-growing Japanese steel company, and he wanted me to facilitate meetings of a committee charged with helping supervisors manage the growth. On the heels of that engagement, another of Sol's directors, the head of a publishing company, asked for help improving their process for preparing sales managers to work in the United States. Through yet another of Sol's directors, I worked with the International Red Cross in Tokyo on a campaign to counteract the marketing success of Western manufacturers of baby formula. To the dismay of health officials, and to the detriment of both babies and mothers, Japanese women were buying the sales pitch that nursing was old-fashioned and abandoning it.

These projects thrilled me. I could practically feel new synapses growing in my brain. For the first time, it occurred to me that I might have more professional choices than teaching and singing.

In 2006, about thirty years after we left Japan, a *New Yorker* cartoon by Victoria Roberts pictured a bewildered man watching from his easy chair as a woman, his wife I presumed, coat on, suitcase packed, says breezily as she heads for the door, "I'm going to France—I'm a different person in France." I understood that woman entirely. I was a different person in Japan.

My friends in Japan were fascinated by my consulting engagements, but Peter wasn't interested. His flare-ups came more often now, and the list of people he was angry with included about half our friends and several Nichibei staff. I often woke in the middle of the night, his outbursts replaying in my mind.

We'd been in Japan four years, and now I told him I wanted to go back to Boston at the end of the term. He argued, but I stood firm. In the end, we booked our flights and gave Nichibei three months' notice.

A couple of weeks before our departure, Peter came home and told me he didn't want to leave after all. He'd just cancelled our reservations and cashed in the irreplaceably low-priced open-dated tickets I'd insisted we buy as a condition for going to Japan in the first place.

"How could you do that!" I started to yell, but I stopped myself. The betrayal. The autocratic action. The forfeited low ticket price. The jobs we'd already given up. The impending termination of our visas. As I lined up my arguments in my mind, the whole way I was thinking felt too familiar. I'd fought with Peter for years by making a logical case, and it had never worked.

The amount of time I had to work at Nichibei to maintain my visa had limited my availability for consulting, but I'd still managed to accumulate some money. Abandoning my fight voice, I told him calmly but resolutely that Ellen and I were going home as planned, whether or not he decided to join us. The next morning, as I was leaving for the ticket office, he called out that I should get him a ticket too.

By the time we set out for Boston, we'd been away five years. I was frantic to get back home. Our marriage was badly frayed, we had a two-year-old, and I was four months pregnant.

— 9 —
TEACUPS

PICTURE IT. BACK FROM JAPAN more than a year. Me, home with an infant at my breast and a toddler at my knee. Him, once a teacher, once an assistant dean, now sporadically driving a cab and earning little. Our marriage, unraveling back in Japan, now even more ragged. I saw the lay of it, but not the fix.

My hunger for rest made it easy to dismiss the marriage trouble. We need sleep, I thought. Sleep and money. That's all.

Peter went on interviews and each time came back saying the work was beneath him, the boss a jerk, the company a joke and went back to driving his cab.

"No one knows Boston streets like I do," he said.

A search firm he was working with cut off all ties. Over time, a rabbi, a neighbor, and a cousin each pulled me aside.

"Peter seems a little . . . well, it's just . . ."

"He's not quite . . . I mean . . . not to pry, but . . ."

"Something isn't . . . so, is he okay?"

Sleep, I thought. And money. Understandable.

I delighted in my babies, wallowed in them, but I was so lonely. In September, I heard about a good chorus and suddenly felt the bone-deep despondency of not singing. My audition went well, and at the first rehearsal, there was Frieda Ployer, a colleague from my old Boston school system days, with an empty chair right next to her. She drove me home, then again the next week, then started picking me up too. We became good friends, though an odd pair. Frieda was fifty-five. I was thirty. She was a product of New York City; I, of Indiana. She was a scientist turned educator, an intimate of composers and artists, a woman with curiosity, verve, savvy. She was exotic and fervid, an Auntie Mame, and I . . . I was exhausted.

Another important friendship would start in that chorus. Joyce had a beautiful soprano voice and sang with great joy. There was a cheeriness about her, and she always seemed so unruffled. I wanted to know her, to be around someone so self-possessed and lighthearted, but she and I sat on opposite sides of the room, and I didn't see a way to meet her.

Rehearsal was well underway one week when Joyce ran in late. The only empty seat near the door was next to me, and she slid into it. "I was all ready to leave when my two-year-old peed on me," she whispered. I flipped over the hem of my skirt to reveal an oily stain, compliments of Ellen, and murmured, "Peanut butter." Pee and peanut butter. That's all it took. Joyce and I became close friends, and so did our daughters.

Frieda came for dinner one night, and, as always when she was there, we were long and festive at the table. Peter reached for his vitamin, and Ellen asked, "What's that for?"

"I don't always have time to eat right," he told her, and she, three years old, said, "And that gives you more time?"

We laughed with the whoops of the utterly besotted. Frieda and I were still grinning when we left for a movie. The film was good, and we were in high spirits on the way home.

When I got out of her car, she leaned toward the open passenger window and said, "I want to ask you at some point, but not tonight—why are you staying with Peter?"

And she drove off.

She never brought it up again. I tried to answer her question for myself and couldn't. A year passed before I accepted that this was itself an answer.

When I told him, he was amenable.

"The girls are most important," I said. "We mustn't frighten them or put them in the middle."

"Right," he said. "Absolutely."

We agreed to separate gently, not in a shoot-out. We wouldn't be like those ones who snared their kids in the barbed wire of it all, who shredded each other and ate their own insides. Besides, what was there to battle over? No savings, no house, not even a car. He said he'd pay child support. I said I'd get a job. Simple. Smart. Civilized.

"Good," we said, and we got up and went to different rooms.

We made lists of who would keep what and figured out when we'd each have the girls. I found a job and sitters and started working. He wanted to stay in the house we were renting, and I found an apartment and signed a lease.

"We'll jointly tell the girls," we said, and we practiced what we'd say.

Close to my move, we called them to the living room. They climbed onto the couch, and we pulled up two chairs. Ellen was four and Jeanie almost two.

"We have something to tell you," I said.

I looked to Peter to speak, but he folded his arms, raised his chin, and fixed his eyes on the ceiling. I faltered and then went on.

"Daddy and I . . ."

I kept looking to Peter to say what we'd prepared, to give the girls a sign that he and I were united in this, but each time I paused, he turned his chair a little more away from us.

"So you'll have one house with me and one with Daddy, and we'll both take care of you," I finished.

Peter stood and went upstairs, having said not a word.

Ellen sat still and somber. Jeanie was unsettled and fidgety. Then Ellen said, "Read us a story," and Jeanie eagerly scooted over to make room for me between them. I picked up a book and joined them on the couch.

The house got increasingly airless. Peter and I barely spoke to each other unless the girls were in the room, and then our voices were tinny and overbright. At the last minute, he said he wouldn't be home when we moved out. He'd leave the night before and come back after we'd gone. I was surprised but, honestly, relieved. It was so draining, pretending for the girls that things were easy between us.

By now my father had moved to Vermont, and I asked him to help me move. I was worried about the girls and frightened about what might be in store for us, and the challenges of the move itself were beyond me. My dad wasn't what you'd call a nurturer, but he had a four-door pickup truck and some extra furniture and would know what to do if a leg broke off a table.

"Thank goodness," he'd said, when I told him about the divorce. "I was afraid you were calling to say you're pregnant."

Of course it would pour on moving day. Extravagantly unfazed by mere weather, my dad was out at the curb throwing a plastic tablecloth over the things in the open bed of the truck. He was yelling something to me, but up on the porch, struggling with a box going pulpy from the rain, I couldn't make out his words. He came and scooped up the soggy box.

"I was saying I passed a yard sale on the way down. There was an old rocking chair, and I picked it up for you. It's got a big crack in the seat, but it's sturdy."

Back in the house, he was still exulting about that cracked rocker while he unplugged a lamp and wrapped the cord around its base. The girls stuck close to me but generally seemed to be taking things in stride.

"Let's put Lamby and these other guys in a bag so they stay dry in the truck," I was saying, when a barrage of boots pounded up the porch steps. Two policemen charged through the front door and stood shoulder to shoulder in front of it, like a wall blocking the way out. Absurdly, a song popped into my head. "*So high you can't go over it, so low you can't go under it. . . .*" My memory is clear: I was knee-high to those cops.

My father lowered the lamp and straightened slowly, empty hands up by his shoulders, palms out, classic hands-up position. I was the one the cops had come looking for, and there I was, a weary woman armed with a plastic bag of stuffed animals and held in place by two little girls gripping my legs.

From another town, at 2 a.m., Peter's lawyer had wakened a judge and sworn that Peter had just learned that in his absence I was sneaking away with tots and treasure—incredibly, accusing me of the stunt my mother had pulled on my father. The cops had guns and papers, and it was the papers they whipped out. A restraining order commanded me to stay put and appear in court a few days later. In that instant I realized I'd been hoodwinked into a dirty war and had marshaled no defenses.

The officers' dripping slickers were shiny as shields. I knew no words would penetrate, and yet I said, "That's not true. He even helped me pack." I added, inanely, "My father drove five hours to get here."

"If you try to leave, we have to stop you," one of them said.

My father, I knew, was revving up, dangerously confident he could fix this.

"Here, Dad," I said, and I swung Jeanie to his chest. "The girls shouldn't see this. Why don't you play with them in the truck."

The cops nodded and made space for them to leave. I wrapped Jeanie's raincoat around her and helped Ellen with hers.

"It's okay," I assured her. "I just have to talk to these men for a few minutes."

She took my father's hand and looked up at him. "Do you have more chocolate in the truck?" she asked.

After they left, the officers blocked the door again. "This is serious," one said. He held out the restraining order, and I took it.

The cruiser was still in the driveway when I went to retrieve the girls. I opened the back door of the truck to help them out, then suddenly, without thought or plan, I dived in.

"Drive!" I screamed.

My dad tore off with the truck door still open. On my knees on the back seat, watching the cops through the rear window, I leaned out dangerously far to pull it shut. The police backed out of the driveway and floored it, hard on our tail.

"Left!" I shrieked. "Then straight!"

The cruiser was gaining. Cars gave way to the siren and soon it was right behind us.

"Next right! Faster!"

My dad was whistling, maddeningly enjoying this. The girls looked up at me, huge-eyed and silent. The cops were so close I could see their scowls. Suddenly I remembered the guns and ducked down.

"Go! Go!" I shrieked.

And then the police just stopped. An untrained fugitive, by dumb luck I'd taken us into another county. My new apartment was three blocks beyond their reach.

Unloading the truck was quick. I'd abandoned nearly everything back at the house. Now I wondered, Had I closed the door behind me? My dad set up the beds and headed out to buy groceries and diapers.

"I got it, I got it!" he barked, when I told him yet again how to avoid crossing back into the old county.

I took both girls into Ellen's bed with me and wrapped my arms around them.

"This is your new room," I said.

A bed, a crib, three cartons on a bare floor.

"I'll tell you a new story."

When they fell asleep, I slipped into the living room and just made it to the cracked rocker, where I started shaking so hard its frame bruised my arm. I shook in that chair for two days while things came and went. Tea, a blanket, now and then a girl in my lap. My dad left for Vermont and, wobbly, I rose, shaking internally now but mightily, thinking equally about avoiding jail and getting pretty curtains for the girls.

Before I could cook, I had to buy a pot. Before I could shower, I had to buy a towel. My friend Joyce brought over toys, books, and clothes from her own daughters' things. As I cut sandwiches into triangles for Ellen and squares for Jeanie, hung their new curtains, read them stories, and played endless games of Hokey Pokey, every voice in the building's vestibule stopped my breath. The snap of handcuffs was so real in my mind, I could feel cold metal on my wrists. The court date was still two days away, and any second now, I was sure, the Norfolk County cops would have the Suffolk County cops come get me. What a mercy it would have been if I'd known that knock would never come.

On my fourth night in the new apartment, I woke up frantic in the blackness. I'd dreamt that Peter had stolen the girls and taken them to Israel or Japan, places where he had connections. I ran to their room and almost cried out when I saw their two curly heads and heard their rhythmic breathing. First thing the next morning, I called the State Department.

"My husband might try to take my daughters out of the country," I said. "Can you block him from getting them passports?"

"Sure," said the guy.

He took down all our names and my contact information and said someone would notify me if a passport application came through for either child. The call took five minutes and was too easy to be reassuring, but it was a straw to grasp when I needed one.

Who'd rewired my husband? His lawyer, I suspect, that zealot from Fathers for Justice or whatever they were called. I can just see him, with his comb-over and plaid suit, when Peter walked in. I can hear his call to war.

"She'll get your kids, your money. They always do, the women. Try to see your little girl—how old did you say?—try to see your little two-year-old, wanting her papa, and bang! Restraining order. Those judges, suckers for the women."

And then, after pausing for Peter to soak it all in, "But I can help you."

I can see Peter, so facilely recruited, so ready to defend his island, fight on beaches, in fields, streets and hills, and never surrender. And I can see the spikey yellow thought-bubble over the lawyer's head: "Got one!"

But maybe it wasn't his lawyer. Despite our daily calls, our lunches out, maybe it was Blanche, Peter's mother, my friend.

Peter's turbulent mother. My ex-friend.

Blanche was a loud-talking, fast-walking exclamation point with red hair and regal bearing. When she was dressed up and entered a room, you knew she was someone. When she was in a bathrobe at the kitchen table, ditto. She died in 2005, and my girls miss her. One named a child after her and gave a moving elegy at the naming ceremony.

Everything in that elegy was true, but it wasn't complete. Blanche could certainly be warm and generous. That side of her had made me a queen when our apartment burned down.

But coiled inside her was a fighter ready for war. With her arm around my waist, she'd once yelled at Peter's father, "Don't you say anything against my Marsha," when he hadn't said a thing. Yet, when I confided in her that I hoped Peter would go to counseling with me, she stopped cold, faced me square on, and said, "Counseling's not for Peter. You need to learn how to live with an extraordinary man."

I was the mother of her grandchildren. Ellen had Blanche's posture; Jeanie, her chuckle. Still, she would attack. I'd left the clan, and the girls were half-clan now.

"Listen," she'd tell her son, perverting everything she'd liked about me, "she's good with words, that one. She'll twist everything you say. Listen to me. The girls adore her. The judge might ask them who they love more. Yes, I'm telling you, judges do that. You'll lose everything. You have to block this before it starts."

His lawyer . . . his mother . . . I think back now and realize Peter hadn't needed much of a push from anyone. He wasn't one for nuances. Things were good or bad, right or wrong, and people were unconditionally in or out. Perhaps I should have known he'd fight crazy, but I didn't. And though others later said they'd foreseen it, no one had warned me.

Teacups? He wanted the teacups? We'd bought them with little thought during our last weeks in Japan. They were cheap but back home would look exotic and make good gifts. His lawyer was reading from a list I knew well.

"There's a set of twelve teacups, your honor, mementoes of their time abroad. My client wants six of them."

"Tell the judge he can have the teacups," I whispered to my lawyer.

His lawyer repeated, "A treasured keepsake, your honor."

"I don't care about the teacups," I whispered again.

My lawyer stood up. "Your honor, we move to dismiss."

"Dismiss, counselor? On what grounds? She defied a restraining order."

"Your honor, counsel is reading from an agreement on the division of household goods that the parties jointly drew up weeks ago. It proves the restraining order was fraudulently obtained."

Case dismissed, simple as that. I wasn't going to jail! I hugged my lawyer, ecstatic. Outside, practically dancing to her car, I said, "I really don't care about those teacups. He can have them."

She whirled to face me. "Would you just forget about those teacups! I don't think you understand what you're into here."

– 10 –

YOU MAY ASK

"**H**EY! WELCOME BACK! HOW WAS your vacation?" my colleagues asked.

On my week off I'd run from the police and the man who'd set them on me, sat in shock for two days in a cracked rocker, talked to my lawyer from payphones until my new phone was installed, lined up care for my daughters in case I was jailed, been exonerated by a judge I still thought was just, and, at the agreed time, gone back to the old house for my belongings and found Peter out and the locks changed.

"I moved," I answered. "It was nice to have the time off to settle in."

The girls and I adjusted to our new life. Jeanie and I dropped Ellen off at nursery school and went to the playground or did errands until it was time to pick her up. At five the sitter came, and I left for work. I called at bedtime to say goodnight, and when I got home, I sat in their room for a while with a cup of tea, watching them sleep in the dimness of their nightlight.

On the weekends the girls were with Peter, I was lonely for them and didn't know how to fill the time. What was I supposed to do after the laundry and grocery shopping were done? But soon those weekends were spoken for. I spent them babysitting other people's children.

In the run-up to our divorce hearing, Peter and his mother had started showing up at my apartment while I was at work and banging on the door. They'd upset the girls, angered my neighbors, and intimidated my sitters. Blanche once talked her way in. Bizarrely, she pulled out a camera and took pictures of my bathroom. "I'm going to show the judge her crummy housekeeping," she told my unnerved sitter. "She's not fit to raise children." And with that, she'd left, leaving it to the sitter to calm her crying granddaughters.

One after another, my sitters quit. Friends could pinch-hit only so much, and so I joined a babysitting pool. On weekends, when my girls were with their father, I took a lot of babysitting assignments to rack up points I could cash in for sitter emergencies.

Finally, when we were legally divorced, Peter and Blanche stopped making trouble at my apartment, but this wasn't a sign of peace. Peter started taking me to court on invented charges. Each time, I countersued for delinquent child support. Each time, his charges against me were dismissed. Each time, he was found in contempt for nonpayment. Occasionally he'd write me one week's check and hand it to me there in the courtroom, but he never followed it with another or paid the ordered arrears. Legal fees cost me more than I gained, but if I didn't appear at these hearings, Peter would win his suit by default.

Under attack by Peter and his mother, I felt again the long-ago fear that trouble could strike at any time from any direction. For seven years I'd eaten normally and easily kept off the weight I'd lost. Now I made a cruel discovery. My eating disorder wasn't cured but had merely been in remission. Even knowing this wild eating would hurt me, I chomped and swallowed as though force-fed by an external power. In less than a year I gained back twenty of the pounds I'd lost seven years earlier, and I wore them for eighteen months.

One afternoon, an hour before Peter was to bring the girls back, I was cooking dinner and singing along with the radio when the phone rang.

"This is the State Department," a young man said. "Your husband applied for passports for your daughters, and we have a notation to call you before issuing."

My heart thundered as though *I* were inside *it* and not the other way around. This man was way too young to handle this. A "notation to call you" was too flimsy.

"Ma'am? Are you there?"

I spoke low and slow. "Do not issue those passports."

"Yes ma'am. I understand."

"How can we be certain they'll be blocked?" I asked, saying "we" to pull him into my fold, a fellowship of those with a stake in this.

"You can be certain," he said, his "you" putting me firmly back on my own.

Four hours later, the girls still weren't home. In my head, I tore through the door and ran to Peter's, his mother's, bus stations, the airport. But in real life, an overwhelming lassitude fell on my body with the weight of a mountain. Only my hands had energy, dialing number after number. There was no social media, no way to mobilize action. My lawyer was away, and her answering machine was full. The police told me it was too soon to consider the girls missing. The courthouse phones rang hollowly. I kept calling Peter and his mother but heard just dead ringing in both places. Fear curdled my stomach until I couldn't tolerate even water, and I whimpered in the night.

In the morning my body could again move, but there was nowhere to go. I was afraid to leave the house in case the girls came back, and I called in sick at work. I paced. I dialed. My lawyer's answering machine was still full. The day shift police echoed the night shift: too soon for a missing persons report. Finally, someone answered at the courthouse, but when I tried to get out my story, he cut me off, told me to call my lawyer, and hung up.

On the third day, Peter called and told me where I would find the girls.

You may ask, How could a man who defied every child support order not face repercussions; a man who intimidated my household not be forced to stop? A father who'd kidnapped his daughters, changed his mind, left them alone on a busy street corner and then called to tell me where to find them— how could such a man be allowed more time alone with them? There's a simple two-word answer. Judge Samuel.

I saw Judge Samuel hector a woman from his high throne until she burst into tears, then turn in his magisterial robes and say to her husband, "Jesus, no wonder you want to get rid of her."

Cops on my tail, with sirens and guns? Trivial. Judge Samuel was armed with the law, his law, which he meted out with his breathtaking leeway. He didn't think it was a problem that Peter yelled through my apartment door, banged on my windows, upset the children, scared off my sitters, and disrupted my work.

"You can solve this yourself," the judge told me. "Just tell the sitter to let him in."

About the girls being kidnapped, he said, "Three days late is hardly kidnapping." About them being left alone, sitting on a curb on a city street, he said, "His mother was on the next block, watching them from her car. That's hardly leaving them alone."

I protested. They were little children, only two and four. They could have run into traffic in a flash, seen but not protected by their block-away grandmother. Judge Samuel said, "For crissake, stop being so dramatic."

Frieda was over, and we sat at the kitchen table, shelling nuts with the girls. A filbert flew out of the nutcracker in my hand, skittered across the floor, banged into a cabinet, and careened off in another direction. The girls loved it and screamed, "Do it again! Do it again, Mommy!"

I grabbed a nut from the bowl and threw it to the floor on purpose. Without missing a beat, Frieda threw one too, and then the four of us were throwing nuts on the floor and laughing so hard we couldn't sit up straight. We were still giggling when we picked them up, and we roared when we found one all the way in the living room.

I put the girls to bed and was smiling when I returned to the living room, but Frieda looked at me very seriously and asked, "What's wrong?"

Peter's harassment. No child support. No prospects.

"You need a new start," she said. "Why don't you apply to Harvard Business School?"

I'd never heard of it and had to ask what a business school was. She settled into her chair.

"They call it the B-school," she began.

I called Sol Mester, who'd left Mattel and was back in the US.

"Great idea! Apply!" he said. "I'll write you a reference!"

By court order, neither Peter nor I could take the girls out of state without the other's permission, so I investigated only local business schools. Six thick packets arrived, one each from Harvard and five others, and by the time I'd gone through them, I was convinced Frieda was right. If I could pull it off, an MBA might let me do work like what I'd glimpsed at Mattel and allow me to support my family without depending on Peter.

Graduates of the other schools seemed generally to return to the same jobs they'd had before business school, typically earning an incremental $250 a year, about $1,200 today. HBS alums, on the other hand, frequently entered new fields and earned bigger salary premiums for their degrees. Ignoring everything I'd ever learned about putting eggs in baskets, I applied only to Harvard Business School.

I dropped my application in the mail the day before the snow fell. Then there was nothing to do but clang shut the postbox and wait. I kept imagining a wan, overburdened young woman in the admissions office, curved over an application on her desk, her hair hanging forward and obscuring her face. I saw my own application, next up in a foot-high pile at her elbow, but I couldn't see beyond that to where she finished the one in front of her and reached for mine. Decisions would be mailed in ten weeks. For that whole time, I'd keep seeing that woman and that pile, mine always next up.

– 11 –

DISCOVERED IN THE SNOW

AN EERIE SILENCE REACHED EVEN into the depths of my sleep, and I awoke disoriented. Boston's city noise, which never went quiet, was completely extinguished. I pushed aside the curtain and saw a snow-covered field with mysterious thin rods, evenly spaced and pointing skyward, outlining a gigantic circle. No footprints led up to it or away. What was this? Stonehenge flashed through my mind, but there'd been no Stonehenge there the night before. There hadn't even been a field. There'd been a circular driveway rimmed with parking spaces.

Slowly, reality registered. During the night, the storm that no one thought would amount to much had landed on the city like an avalanche and buried the parked cars. The mysterious rods were the antennas poking up through the snow.

This was the Blizzard of '78. Roads, hedges, fences, benches—all lay under a car-deep plateau. The radio, announcing the eminently obvious, kept repeating that emergency vehicles were as yet unable to move in many sections of the city, and no private vehicles were allowed on any streets.

My world was impassable, and I had to get to work. I needed the money.

Some high-spirited college kids had tried to dig a path from the door of my apartment building to the street, but they'd given up when they hit a buried Volkswagen. I had no choice. The girls were at Peter's, so I didn't have to think about a sitter. I put on two shirts and two pairs of pants, smeared Vaseline on my face, tied plastic bags over my boots, climbed onto that Volkswagen, and set out on the tops of cars.

Wind-driven ice bits blew into my eyes and blinded me. Car by car, for over an hour, I climbed onto bumpers by feel, scrabbled on my belly from trunks to roofs, and slid on my bottom down windshields to hoods. Ice-glazed drifts in the spaces between cars were shoulder-high, and I flailed around in them until some part of my body struck the next bumper.

Terror came as a vision of Peter leaving the girls outside my locked apartment while I lay dead in a drift. It came as screams from my body—"I need breath! I need rest!"—and my mind screamed back, "If I stop, my muscles won't restart. If I pause to catch my breath, the drifts will close over me."

Two hours. Fingers and feet burning with cold. Clothes soaked, weighing me down. After every third or fourth car, I rested on a roof or a hood, aware of the danger of falling asleep but unable to carry on without pausing to focus my mind and muster my strength.

Three hours. I'd gone less than a mile. The whole way, there'd been no sign of another person and no sounds but my own.

High on its hill, St. Elizabeth's Hospital rose above me, silent and yellow like an ancient pueblo. The place looked as though it had been deserted for centuries.

Its driveway and walks were plowed, but the plowing ended abruptly at the wall of snow where the street began. I slid off the car I was on and went at that snow with knees, fists, elbows, and hips until I broke through to the hospital grounds. Only when I finally stood on the blacktop of the driveway did I emerge from the trial of my body and the babel of my brain. Shaking with cold and the sudden lack of struggle, I made my way up the long steep driveway and around to the front door, hearing in the portentous silence only the thwacking of my boots and the labor of my own breathing.

I expected to find the wings of the revolving doors broken from their shaft, the lobby dark and chairs every which way, but when I got to the entrance, the lights were on and there were people inside. A few guys in scrubs were asleep on the floor. A man in a suit lay across several chairs, eyes closed, foot twitching. Two orderlies leaned against the information booth and talked quietly.

A nurse hurried my way, but I waved to her that I was fine. In my sodden clothes, I lumbered to a restroom, peeled off my extra layers, and dropped them to the floor, where water seeped out of them. The plastic bags had shredded away, and my boots were full of snow. Swaddling my bare feet in wet paper towels, I shuffled down a back hall to a room with two mismatched desks, a metal table, harsh lighting, and a leggy philodendron. It was the anteroom of the nursing director's suite. The chairs around the table were empty. On one of the desks, neatly stacked folders and an empty coffee cup waited for a secretary who couldn't get in. The plant needed water.

Black scrapes on the linoleum showed where some file cabinets had been moved to make room for a part-time typist.

I was that typist.

Three years earlier I'd been a consultant in Tokyo. I had corporate experience on my resume, but Japan wasn't yet hot in the business world. When I talked about my experience there, one prospective employer after another dismissed it so readily, I could have been talking about flower arranging. Like all the others before her, the hospital's human resources screener had put my resume aside with hardly a glance. She offered me a typing test, and because I typed ninety words a minute, I finally got hired. The pay was $75 a week, and the girls and I were on food stamps.

St. Elizabeth's was a designated response center for regional emergencies. TV and radio stations were giving out our number, but staff who'd been trained to handle the calls couldn't get in. The office was deserted except for Jane, a nursing supervisor who was alternating between answering the hotline and tending to the wards. She was sitting at my desk, just hanging up the phone, when I walked in.

Blotchy from the cold, feet wrapped in paper, holding that drippy bundle of woebegone clothes, I must have looked like I'd crawled up through a drain. We were both so exhausted we just stared at each other. Jane spoke first.

"How'd you get here?"

"I walked," I said.

She raised an eyebrow.

"On top of the cars," I added.

She jumped up and pointed to the phone on my desk, which had become the hotline.

"Log all calls. Write everything down. Say you'll get back to them. I'll keep swinging by to give you answers. Page me for emergencies."

And she was gone.

I paged her for calls from a nursing home out of food and an injured man trying to stop his bleeding, but I didn't need to page for a call from a frantic mother trapped with her newborn son in an apartment without electricity. She sounded young. A teen she might have been. At the start of the storm, the hospital where she'd delivered had handed her the infant and a bag of formula and sent her on her way. Now the formula was gone and there was no way to get more. Her baby was hysterical, and she didn't know how to breastfeed.

In Tokyo, after Ellen was born, I'd become an instructor for La Leche League, a support group for nursing mothers. Now, speaking very calmly, I coached this young woman until she felt her son latch and her milk let down. While he nursed, she kept murmuring, "He's so beautiful. He's just so beautiful." Finally well fed, he slept in her arms. The peace of it made her weep.

If she wanted, I said, she could call back when he was hungry again and we'd go through it again together. She did call back, and she did fine. Once she asked, "I should switch sides now, right?" and I told her, "You're doing so well. You know just what to do."

I often think of her and her boy, how terrified she was, and how brave. I hope there's a healthy man somewhere who knows this story of his third day alive, how his mother soothed him and fed him and, even in a dark apartment, saw his beauty.

Staff were sparse and flagging. Coverage was improvised on the fly, and surgeries were rescheduled. With vending machines long empty, we pilfered snacks from the desks of absent colleagues. In a friend's desk down the hall, I struck gold with two Kit Kats. I polished one off standing right there and saved the other for Jane. She was the only nursing supervisor on duty when there should have been three. Prevented by the snow from going home the previous evening, she'd just kept on working, by now for three straight shifts of overseeing the hotline on top of a triple case load.

I'd come to learn how she wanted me to handle the most basic calls, and instead of paging her, I started dealing directly with the fire department, civil defense, and the Red Cross on these. The first time she looked at the phone log and found I'd already checked off some entries, she snatched it from my hands, grilled me, and then said, "Okay, fine. Page if you need me," and ran out again.

Later I did page, when a generator at another hospital failed and the dialysis machines of thirteen patients abruptly stopped.

"Oh sweet Jesus!" she cried.

I told her I'd arranged emergency transport for the patients and dialysis staff and had a maintenance crew standing by, waiting to see if she wanted them to set up a makeshift ward and auxiliary generator in our auditorium. After a beat she said, "Tell them to set it up stat," and headed for the auditorium.

"Good job with that dialysis plan," she said the next time she came by. "Let me see what you've done since then." From that point on, with her blessing, I handled most of the calls on my own.

My daughters were still snowed in at Peter's, and I covered the hotline for three days and three nights. I imagine I took catnaps, but I recall only a special energy running through me that I hadn't felt since Tokyo: the birr of working, of heightened attention and hard thinking.

When I left, the streets were walkable. Wired with both exhaustion and exhilaration, I paced around my living room until I could sleep. My girls came back the next afternoon, and I stayed home with them a few days, after which midnight struck and Cinderella was again a typist.

It couldn't have been more than a month later when a man I knew only from his portrait in the lobby walked in. Immediately I rose and faced him across my desk, practically standing at attention. It was William Skerry, the hospital president, with my resume plucked from Human Resources and in his hand.

"Tell me about your work in Japan," he said, and he pulled up a chair. We talked for half an hour. As he stood to leave, he said, "Let's get you off that typewriter, shall we?"

If residents funded by Medicaid left their nursing homes for long enough, even to be hospitalized, the nursing homes were allowed to give their slots to someone else. This meant a patient could become homeless, stranded in the hospital for weeks or even months due to the shortage of Medicaid nursing home beds—a catastrophe for the patient and a strain on the hospital. One case on this ward, two on that, and the count at St. Elizabeth's had climbed to more than twenty such patients.

Now I was a project manager with a private office and a raise to $87 a week. The problem of stranded Medicaid patients was mine to solve.

By then we all knew that when the blizzard crashed onto the region, 3,500 drivers on Route 128 had watched through their windshields as their own burials progressed; that three thousand of them had abandoned their vehicles and escaped, and that many who didn't had died in theirs; that a ten-year-old had perished in a drift just three feet from his front door and wasn't found until his boot emerged in the melt three weeks later.

It was sheer luck that I survived that brainless escapade on the tops of cars on deserted, snowbound streets. It frightened me that I could be so reckless, and I vowed never to tell my girls what I'd done, lest they admire it.

Of course I was grateful for the new job, but I never felt celebratory or fully comfortable about it, knowing it had come to me from what was, to so many others, a profound catastrophe.

Ellen's nursery school reopened, and I hauled the kids there on a borrowed Flexible Flyer. It was hard going. Trampled but not shoveled, the sidewalks were craggy with cracked, frozen snow and littered with ice divots that jerked the sled around and stopped the runners like gravel. Hardly able to hold on with their mittens, the girls slid around in their puffy snowsuits and sometimes slipped off the sled entirely.

We finally got Ellen dropped off, and Jeanie and I went on to the supermarket. Traffic other than emergency vehicles was still prohibited, and the shelves hadn't been replenished. A single cabbage was the only fresh produce remaining. Back home, I turned the cabbage into a borscht, put Jeanie back on the sled, and set out to pick up Ellen.

Jeanie had had enough. Her nose was a snot faucet, and she wailed the whole way back to our apartment. Ellen whined,

"She's bothering me!" on a continuous loop. Home was only a few blocks away, but I was on the brink of falling apart. The sidewalk had become an unnerving narrow channel, not much wider than the sled and walled on both sides with shiny hard-frozen snowbanks higher than my head. We could see neither left nor right, but only straight ahead. All landmarks were hidden behind those walls, and I had the creepy sensation of being trapped in a white maze with no sense of direction or distance.

The ice channel turned a corner, and suddenly a couple materialized before us, looking perplexed and altogether like they'd just been beamed from a warmer, kinder place. They appeared to be in their mid-thirties. The woman, Marina, was in a light wool coat, a dress, and—I'm certain, but can this possibly be right?—stockings and heels. Her husband, Michael, was also without boots and wore improbable leather oxfords with a suit and topcoat. Marina's English was better than Michael's, and she explained that they and their daughter, Sasha, had arrived from Russia just a few days earlier. They were staying with a cousin one town over while they looked for an apartment. Michael showed me a rental listing circled on a page torn from the *Boston Globe*, and I saw immediately that they were looking for a realtor's office they thought was nearby but was two miles away.

We were right outside my apartment. The snow and cold were miserable, and there was soup inside. Ignoring everything I'd been warned about letting in strangers, I invited them to join us for lunch. While we ate, Marina described the months-long journey they'd endured to get to the United States, a story that echoed the fraught and risky passage that had brought my grandmother Minnie to America.

Minnie was an orphan, a tiny thing, under five feet and just thirteen when somehow she convinced a shipping agent that she was twenty and her eight-year-old sister was ten, the minimum ages required for an adult and a child to sail away from poverty and pogroms in Mezhyrich, Ukraine, to who-knew-what in Philadelphia, America.

Train after train, way station after way station, they pressed on for more than a year, their group swelling at each stop as a river swells with tributaries. Wait here. Line up there. Show passports. Board another train. . . .

Near the end, in Galicia, they were led to long benches at vast tables laid out with tea, dark bread, and prune jelly. While they were eating, an officious young man tapped Minnie's shoulder and asked to check her passport. "I'll bring it right back," he said, then vanished with it.

She was terrified. She searched for an official, and the best she could find was a Jewish cook who spoke Yiddish. "Little girl," he told her, "You'll never get that passport back, but maybe I can do something." The cook had a buddy, who wrote her a note. Who the buddy was and what the note said, Minnie had no idea, but the emigration authority smoothly assigned the girls to a ship.

"Somehow he fixed it," she told me. "I was written up in places."

"What do you mean, you were written up in places?" I asked. I was fifteen when she told me this story, and it haunted me.

"I was assigned to a ship, that's all," she said, "and we were on the manifest. I got here. I made it through." She waved away the whole thing.

After almost sixty years in America, the passport robbery was as nothing to her. Yet she remembered every detail of that modest meal in Galicia. Her face got dreamy when she spoke of the freshness of the bread, the gratifying warmth of the tea, the luxurious sweetness of the prune jelly. How very hungry those girls must have been.

Now, more than a decade after I learned about the orphaned sisters' journey, Michael and Marina, hungry and cold, were eating bread and hot soup in my apartment, wearing all the clothes they had because their luggage, with its boots and warm coats, hadn't made it onto the plane.

After we ate, I phoned the realtor who'd found me my own apartment, and she got them a place that same day. When they moved in, I gave them a spare chair and a wastebasket from my helter-skelter move. In a matter of hours, we felt like old friends.

It took all the way from February to April for the snow from the blizzard to be largely reduced to wet piles. Daffodils worked their way through the slush to the sun; sidewalks were easy to navigate, and streets were mostly clear. The girls and I hadn't seen Minnie in almost a year, and it felt like this was a good time for her to come. "Invite Michael and Marina," she said, eager to meet my new friends from the old country. "I'll make us a Russian meal."

A feast, she should have said—chicken cutlets, pelmeni, stuffed cabbage, homemade black bread. A huge platter of herring, beets, eggs, and potatoes started things off, and an apple cake, warm from the oven, waited on the kitchen counter. We were tight around my little table. Marina and I sat on one side, with my grandmother and Michael across from us. Jeanie and Ellen squeezed together on one end, and shy little Sasha, not much of an eater, sat at the other and stared at them as they gustily took seconds and thirds.

Years later, Sasha would email me, "When we first arrived, I remember thinking, How terrific America is. No school, and sledding down a highway (Route 9)! I thought, 'That's how every winter is around here!'" By the time she wrote this, she was a Fulbright scholar and a Doctor of Science, but at that dinner, she whispered in self-conscious English, "No thank you," when Marina urged another forkful on her, and, "I am eight years old," when my grandmother asked her age. Otherwise, she worked hard at disappearing in place.

Somehow I missed what started the stir, but suddenly my grandmother and Marina were on their feet, leaning across the table until their foreheads almost touched, and hollering at each other in Russian. Jeanie screamed, "What's the matter? What's the matter?" and looked at me with big eyes. I was alarmed too, until I saw Michael grinning broadly, his head toggling back and forth from his wife to Minnie. Then he and even little Sasha were laughing and yelling, "English! Stop! Talk English!"

My grandmother and Marina had just discovered that Marina's mother, as a young child, had fled with her parents to Kyiv from the same tiny shtetl my grandmother fled from a few years later. That shtetl had been so small and intermarried that, distantly though it might have been, and several times removed, we were surely kin.

My office phone rang, and I reached for it with my right hand while my left annotated a nursing home report on my desk. I hoped this would be a quick call. I had a lot of work to do, and I needed to be home by ten. That was our deal, the trio's and mine. They were three cheerful, responsible teenagers, best friends, whom my daughters and I adored. In a charmed arrangement, I'd hired them as a group. They juggled among themselves, and one of them—the girls and I didn't care which—showed up every day after school to babysit. My part of the compact was to be home on time.

It was that night's sitter calling. "Your husband's here! He's banging on the windows!"

I heard the girls crying, the distant banging, my sitter's distress.

"I'm phoning the police," I said. "I'll call you right back."

I closed my office door and dialed the precinct near my apartment, then called her back. "They're on the way," I said. "I'll stay on the phone with you until they get there and take care of things. You've been perfect. I'm so grateful."

My mouth wittered on while my brain ticked off a crazy checklist. Are the girls okay? I'll lose my job! Where are those police?

"You rest a minute while I talk to the girls," I said. "Then I'll come straight home." The police arrived and escorted Peter off the property. An incident like this hadn't happened in over a year, and now he was at it again. He kept showing up for weeks, and, as I would have done, the trio's mothers forbade their daughters to sit for me anymore.

Michael, Marina, and Sasha had been in their new apartment for six months. Marina, a renowned materials scientist, had quickly found work at Polaroid, but Michael was still taking English lessons. Eventually he'd be a prominent civil engineer here, as he'd been in Russia, but now he became my girls' babysitter. With a deep-voiced man on the other side of the door, Peter finally stopped showing up.

– 12 –

OZ ACROSS THE RIVER

HONESTLY. COULDN'T ANYTHING JUST GO smoothly for once? The date for Harvard's decision passed, then another week, and still I'd heard nothing. Finally, I phoned the admissions office.

"Acceptances went out a week and a half ago," the receptionist said. "Rejections are going out today." Two days later, a slim one-pager arrived, and everybody knows thick is yes, thin is no. I threw the envelope on a table, ran up a flight to my friend Kim's, and sobbed at her kitchen table while she boiled water for tea.

The next day I dropped the unopened letter in the wastebasket but then retrieved it to pick the scab. "Congratulations! We are delighted to inform you . . ." I ran back up to Kim's and burst in on her and her mother, who'd just arrived for a visit.

"I got in!" I cried. I'm going to business school!" Kim screamed and grabbed my hands. The two of us jumped up and down in her tiny entryway and then just stood and looked at each other, disbelieving yet also believing what had just happened and trying to divine everything this could mean.

"Kim," her mother said from the couch, "her hands are shaking. I don't like that shaking, Kim."

There was a dragon at the gate, one with the power to appear as an unremarkable woman in sensible shoes. She was the financial aid officer, she'd have me know, and she'd have none of it, this mewling about small children.

I was short $4,000, about $15,000 in today's money, because my HBS financial aid package covered only the expenses of a single adult, not a family of three.

"We don't consider children," the dragon said. "Loans are based on projected ability to repay, and you're the only earner."

"But they accepted me with the children!" I argued.

"Well they shouldn't have," she snapped.

Her deadline for me to close the gap—the day she'd notify the registrar which financial aid recipients could matriculate—was firm, and she was emphatic that HBS had given me my maximum loan level. I couldn't take on any more debt and would have to find $4,000 in scholarships, grants, or gifts.

The National Potato Council and the American Fire Sprinkler Association offer financial aid. There's aid out there for left-handed people and people with glasses. I—a lefty, a wearer of glasses—pored over eight hundred pages of financial aid catalogs in the Boston Public Library, found sixty-one possibilities, and applied to all of them. A few grants came in, and I reported each to Dragon. On every call, she reminded me of the deadline and the no-more-loans rule. The day before the deadline, I was still $1,500 short.

"Please," I begged, "I've got one more to hear from, and the award date is this week. Just another couple of days." She wouldn't budge. Her deadline passed, and the very next day the award letter arrived.

When I called her, they said she was in a meeting. Until now, I'd left messages for her to call me back, but this time I insisted they go get her. She picked up the phone saying, "I told you . . ."

"I got the $1,500," I interrupted.

"From where?"

"Combined Jewish Philanthropies."

"The whole $1,500?"

"Precisely $1,500."

"Loan or grant?"

"Grant."

"Fine," she said, and she hung up.

Truth be told, it was a loan.

I bought an old Ford that I'd later discover was so rusty, only the paint job kept it car-shaped. My brother Craig lived in Brooklyn at that point, and he drove up and moved the girls and me into graduate student housing. A week later, I dropped Ellen at kindergarten and Jeanie at daycare, then walked across the footbridge over the Charles River to that sparkling Oz on the far bank, the Harvard Business School.

The opening ceremonies were held on the green in front of Baker Library, whose columned front and patrician bell tower endowed the whole campus with an aura of authority. It could have been our graduation instead of our first day, the way the morning's speakers glorified us. As one after another extolled our incomparable selves and the transcendent alumni in whose footsteps we followed, it sank in for the first time how truly astonishing it was that I was in that place. Only a year earlier I'd run away from my own home, chased by the police.

My new classmates and I practically vibrated with the thrill of that perfect day on that perfect lawn. Most of the others were only a few years out of college and looked impossibly young and unfettered. When they were being potty trained, I was hitting puberty; still, many of them had already had real jobs with businessy titles, while I'd taught fifth grade, done a little consulting in Tokyo, and been a part-time typist. Only now did I understand how meager my experience had been and realize how much gold I'd spun out of straw on my application.

But surely the Harvard Business School knew a load of straw when it saw one, so how had I gotten in along with these twenty-four-karat others? After lunch, when copies of the *Harbus News,* the student newspaper, were distributed, a set of numbers under the headline "Class of '80: Best Ever" made everything clear. Ninety percent of the class was younger than me. Women were overwhelmingly outnumbered by men. The number of students from the Midwest was so small, it wasn't even listed. No wonder they'd accepted me. They'd needed me for ballast.

Every morning, I dropped off the girls and walked across the river. Three times a day for two years, about five hundred times in all, my classmates and I struggled to solve real-life problems that had been faced by real-life managers. Five hundred times, working with the same constraints and imperfect data that the real managers had had, we figured out what we'd have done in their shoes, explained our decisions, and described how we'd recover if we were wrong. Five hundred times we disagreed, improved our analyses, and refined our judgments. This was the vaunted Case Method, a great education, but grueling in the getting.

Classes were thirty-five hours a week. It took me another thirty-five to prep the week's cases, and—my own inviolable rule—I did no homework between picking up the girls in the afternoon and putting them to bed. Often, I woke at 3 a.m. with my head on the kitchen table and Ellen, half sleepy curlyhead, half hall monitor, tapping my elbow with her little index finger and saying, "Mommy, you fell asleep on your cases again."

They told me I was the first single parent at HBS with kids in tow, and I learned right from the start that this would get me no special consideration. In exercises intended to teach us to write "business English," we were given a case at the end of the day and had to analyze it, write it up and drop our work through a specific mail slot back on campus by midnight. I couldn't get a sitter at that hour, and I wouldn't leave my five- and three-year-olds alone while I did a late-night dash across the river to the business school. When I approached the professor with some possible workarounds, he dismissed them out of hand. Employing similarly flawed logic to that used by medical schools claiming thirty-hour shifts would "train" medical students to go without sleep, he insisted his methodology was training us to put family needs aside, because our future employers would demand it.

Meanwhile, Peter stepped up his court filings to once a month. His complaints were still unfounded. Every one of them still got dismissed by the judge, but I had to show up in court each time, and that meant missing a full day of classes.

One day at a time, despite inflexible professors and Peter's harassment, the first year was finally over. My degree was now just one year away.

At the end of the summer before my final year, I had two weeks of exquisite laziness with picnics, ladybugs, and two little barefoot girls in bathing suits. In the middle of this luxury, just barely announcing itself, a small pain started up in my back. Ten days before the beginning of classes, I got out of bed one morning, screamed with pain, and collapsed to the floor. My legs were useless. My back was searing.

The girls were in their room, too sound asleep to hear me calling. Above me, the telephone cord dangled from my bed table, and I reached up and gave it little tugs, inching the phone to the table's edge. On the last tug, I just had time to protect my head with my arms before the base and receiver of that heavy rotary phone fell on me.

Dr. William Kaden, director of health services at the business school, had gone in early that day, and he answered the phone himself. With compassion and certainty, he told me help would arrive soon and called an ambulance.

Utterly unconsoled by my shouted reassurances, Ellen and Jeanie stood in tears on the sidewalk with my friend Joyce and cried out for me as the ambulance doors closed. When I woke up, I was in Harvard's Stillman Infirmary, in a bed cranked up to hold my torso in a semi-sitting position. My legs were suspended out in front of me in midair, strapped to ropes that hung from a system of pulleys and weights attached to a frame high above my bed. I had no memory whatsoever of getting trussed up like that.

Dr. Kaden was in a chair at my bedside. "You have a slipped disc," he said. "These weights are pulling your legs away from your spine to increase the space between the vertebrae. That should allow the disc to work its way back where it belongs. The orthopedist estimates it will take about a week." A decade later, this kind of long-term traction for back problems would be discredited, but at that time it was accepted practice. Drawbacks it had, but an advantage too. In traction, I had almost no pain. Out of it, even the smallest movement was excruciating.

The girls stayed at Joyce's for a few days, then with Michael and Marina for a few more. From then on, I was on the phone every day, trying to line up people the girls knew who could take them until I was discharged. Blanche hung up as soon as she heard my voice. Peter also hung up, but not before he delivered a long speech that started with, "I won't be taken for granted every time something comes up."

All day, all night, the weights pulled on my legs. My torso was kept on a slant too low for actually sitting up and too high for sleeping. I was miserable and wanted only to be back home with my girls, but by week's end, the rogue disc hadn't budged. A second week of traction was ordered.

The most painful part of each day was my phone call to my daughters. Of course, my sudden and dramatic disappearance had frightened them, and being shuttled from friend to friend was making things worse. They said almost nothing when we were on the phone, but they got hysterical when it was time to hang up. As soon as it was clear I'd be in the hospital another week, my lawyer threatened Peter with legal action if he didn't take the girls. Ultimately, he did, and they were at least in a familiar place.

Now classes were about to start, and my friends from first year mobilized. One claimed to be me at registration, enrolled me in my courses, and signed my name. Fortunately, she wasn't asked to show her ID. Others assured each professor I'd show up soon and faithfully brought me class notes and assignments.

The traction went on through August and into September. Peter enrolled Ellen in first grade and Jeanie in daycare in the town where he lived, giving them some routine at last. Once, he brought them to Stillman to visit me, but they were so upset when it was time to leave, he wouldn't bring them again and dismissed my argument that regular visits would be reassuring and help them adjust to these new circumstances. "You'll just upset them," he said. "A clean break will be better." Soon he wouldn't let me talk to them on the phone. I missed them desperately and was sure they believed I'd abandoned them. I was inconsolable.

During this period, Peter filed a complaint against me over some issue I've now forgotten. Dr. Kaden tried hard to intervene, but the judge denied a postponement. Not even trying to hide their shock that such a thing could happen, infirmary staff unstrung me, got me into a wheelchair, and positioned me as best they could across the back seat of my lawyer's car, on my back, with pillows under my torso and knees. By the time we reached the courthouse, I was in a stupor from the pain. It took my lawyer and a stranger she flagged down more than twenty minutes to get me out of the car and onto the walkway, where we learned that the wheelchair we'd been assured would be waiting for us didn't exist.

Sitting on a courtroom bench was out of the question, and so was standing. Whispering profuse apologies for the lack of options, a solicitous court officer helped me lie down on a patch of floor between the back wall of the courtroom and an empty desk, out of view and out of the way. No sooner had I gotten down than Judge Samuel called a halt to the case before him and boomed across the courtroom that if I didn't get up and take a seat, he'd hold me in contempt. Angrily, he cut off my lawyer's attempted explanation and made the entire court wait while she and the officer, practically carrying me, helped me up and got me to a bench. The pain was agonizing. I was nauseated and afraid I would black out. When our case was called, the judge insisted I get up and join my lawyer in the front of the room, though it wasn't protocol. When finally I got there, our hearing lasted less than a minute. Making it clear that the law gave him no choice, Samuel threw out Peter's complaint.

Medically, things were at a standstill. The traction wasn't helping, and the orthopedist wanted to give it more time. It was late September, a full month into the semester, and I hadn't been to any classes. This was serious. Class participation in case analyses counted for half our grade, and I was at real risk of flunking out.

"How will I ever get to class if my legs are hanging from the ceiling?" I whined to Joyce. A few days later, she stood at the foot of my bed with Bob, a close friend of hers who ran a major Boston medical center. A technician he'd brought along from their prosthetics lab methodically worked his way around my bed, measuring the incline of my torso, the angles of my thighs to my hips and my calves to my thighs—all the angles the traction imposed on my body—and jotted the numbers on a stick figure in his notebook. When done, it looked too fittingly like a bug on its back.

"We'll put our heads together on this at the lab," Bob promised. "You'll hear from us soon."

A couple of weeks later, he returned with a fantastical machine. A heavy, old-fashioned wooden wheelchair, consigned to storage years earlier when lighter models replaced it, was back in action, retrofitted to hold my body in the traction position. The backrest now slanted backwards from the seat, which had a new wooden wedge bolted to it to keep my knees higher than my bottom. Leg rests, higher still, held my feet out in front of me, pointing skyward. Clunky, preposterous, and heavy as hell, this was my starship.

No charge, no paperwork. "Just let me know when you're done with it," Bob said, "and I'll send someone to pick it up."

Dr. Kaden wrote an order for a wheelchair van to take me to the business school campus twice a week. "Be sure to tell them it's not a regular wheelchair," he told the nurse. "They'll have to bring extra straps." That old wooden wheelchair alone had weighed more than sixty pounds. With the added customizations and my weight on it, I couldn't possibly get it moving on my own, but my business school friends solved that problem by organizing a rotation to meet the van when it arrived on campus and push me where I needed to go.

What a figure we must have cut—I, with my contorted body, being paraded around in a jerry-rigged litter like some Dr. Seuss pasha. As our little procession made its way around campus, students I didn't know came up to investigate, and several added themselves to the corps of volunteers who pushed me from class to class and brought notes and assignments to me in the infirmary.

When I rolled into classes, I was surrounded like a celebrity, or maybe like a zoo animal. Though the professors had heard from my friends that I was laid up, I think the severity of my situation registered only when they saw me and took in the impressive effort and clever carpentry it had taken to get me there. That tangy first day back revitalized my logy mind. I felt kinetic and strong beyond the reality of my bed-weakened muscles. For the first time, I believed everything would be fine.

Eventually, though, it was undeniable that the traction wasn't working. Dr. John Shillito, a legendary neurosurgeon, was preparing to retire and taking no new patients, but somehow Dr. Kaden convinced him to see me. Dr. Shillito discovered that my slipped disk was impinging on my sciatic nerve. If I didn't have surgery soon, he said, I might lose my ability to walk.

Back in traction at Stillman, with a week to go before the operation, I desperately needed to hear my daughters' voices, but Peter wouldn't allow it. "This isn't a good time," he said, no matter when I called. I couldn't move him, and I fell into a deep grief, almost unresponsive to those around me. I had nightmares of a scalpel slipping in the doctor's hand and slashing my spinal cord, leaving me permanently confined to a wheelchair that I couldn't move, no longer able to take care of my girls.

When Joyce came to visit, she found me too despondent to talk. The next day she showed up with a lavishly giftwrapped bathrobe, deep rose with white piping, thick and soft. "Believe me," she said. "You'll be walking around after the surgery, and you'll need this."

Michael and Marina offered to go with me to the hospital and be there throughout the surgery. Frieda, who by now had moved to a town a hundred miles away, made the same offer.

"My father's driving down," I told them. "I won't be alone."

A few days later, the traction was unhooked for the last time, and I was rolled into an ambulance for the ride to the Peter Bent Brigham Hospital. In Dr. Shillito's office, dark rectangles on the faded wallpaper showed where his diplomas had hung, and a few open cartons of books waited on the floor to be sealed. The knowledge that he was ready to leave his career behind felt ominous, but when he explained the next day's surgery to my father and me, it was clear he was still very much in the game.

Outside the doctor's office, waiting for a porter to come and wheel me to my room, my father said, "Okay. I'm off. Good luck tomorrow."

"What do you mean, you're off?"

"I have to get back to Vermont," he said. "It's a long drive."

"What are you talking about? The surgery's tomorrow. That's what you're here for."

"I wanted to check out the doctor," my father said. "It looks like you're in good hands." By the time the porter arrived, I was alone.

"Ma-a-arsha . . . Ma-a-arsha . . ." A singsong voice was calling me, and I rose to the surface from a deep and placid place. "It all went fine," a nurse said, slapping the backs of my hands to keep me with her. "Doctor will be in soon to talk to you."

"Can I walk?" I asked her.

"Pretty soon," she said.

"So my legs can walk?"

"Of course your legs can walk, but you're still woozy. We'll have you up soon enough."

Dr. Shillito was upbeat. Things had gone better than he'd hoped. The next day, he said, I'd go back to Stillman to recuperate for a month. In late November I'd go home, and in December I'd start a year of physical therapy.

"Can I walk? Without damaging anything?" I asked.

"Oh, sure, when you're steady on your feet. We'll keep an eye on you for a while here in Recovery and then take you to your room. You'll be walking around by dinner."

My bed was next to the open door to the recovery unit. As soon as he left, I edged my legs over the side of the bed and sat for a minute. Nothing hurt, and I wasn't dizzy. With curtains around my bed providing privacy, I fished some coins from my wallet in the plastic bag of my belongings at the foot of the bed, held my johnny closed with one hand, tightly gripped my IV pole with the other, and, walking very slowly, rolled it out of the recovery room to the payphone down the hall.

When Peter picked up, all I said was, "Let me talk to the girls."

"This isn't a good time. They're about to . . ."

"Get those girls to the phone right now," I ordered, with authority I didn't know I could summon. The next thing I heard was, "Mommy! Hi, Mommy!"

The nurses found me leaning against the phone booth, too drained to move and wishing I'd put on my new robe so I could let go of the johnny.

"I'm fine," I said. "I'm ready to get back in bed. Everything's fine."

– 13 –

HOME COOKING

BACK TO THE DAMN INFIRMARY in another damn ambulance. Another damn wheelchair ride down the same damn hall to the same damn room. This time it was to give me time to heal from the surgery. With the traction apparatus gone, the room looked large and airy, but I was so frustrated I couldn't appreciate the transformation.

Why was I even here? I could walk. I was strong. It was time to get my girls back and time to go be a student.

Big talker. I could walk, but just a little. After three months in bed, my muscles had all the tone of a bag of marshmallows. Three weeks into my four-week recuperation at Stillman, I still had a long way to go. I could sit, but not long enough for a whole class. Most doors were too heavy for me to open. I wouldn't be able to lift Jeanie.

A nurse tried to reassure me. "That's what physical therapy is for," she said, but there was no comfort in that. Adjust to being on my own at home, having the girls back, dealing with school, and, on top of all that, fitting in a year of physical therapy? Impossible.

My body, my family, my resolve, my prospects—not one of these was intact. Normalcy will be a long time coming, I thought, and night after night I lay awake with my mind spinning. I'd finally fall asleep around dawn, just about the time a nurse came in and popped a thermometer in my mouth. Not at all annoyed at being wakened, I'd be grateful for her care, grateful to be touched, even by someone simply checking my pulse.

I'd applied to Brandeis because someone told me to. I'd agreed to a bad marriage because I'd seen no choice. This time, I knew, I had to step up and take charge of my own situation, but I felt so alone and out of resilience. I called my mother and asked her to come help me when I was discharged.

"Oh, you know, that's not my thing," she said.

Instead of help, my father offered advice. "Give the kids to Peter and get on with your career."

My grandmother Minnie called, and I spared her none of my self-pity. "I'm utterly depleted," I told her. "I need every kind of nourishment there is in this world," I think I said. That afternoon, in her little Bronx kitchen, Minnie started cooking. She roasted three chickens, cooked eight different vegetables, baked bread, made stuffed cabbage, kasha, sweet potatoes, chicken soup, vegetable soup, and barley soup and filled her own and several neighbors' freezers with it all.

Craig picked up the food, loaded it in his trunk, and set out to bring it to Boston. On the way, he had to attend a conference in Connecticut, and somehow he convinced the kitchen manager at the venue to store a miscellany of rock-hard plastic containers and aluminum-foiled chicken-shaped objects in the industrial freezer.

A couple of days later, afraid that everything was defrosting, he burst into my hospital room calling out, "Key! Give me your key!" He snatched it from my hand, rushed to my apartment, loaded my freezer and refrigerator, opened the windows, tossed the dead plant, and drove back to the infirmary. "You're all set," he said. "Everything was still frozen. You just need fruit and vegetables and some milk. I'll get them tomorrow, after we have you settled in your apartment."

I was discharged in December, on the last day of classes, and the next day my daughters came home. They'd bounced from friend to friend until their father finally took them. Ellen had started first grade in an unfamiliar school and would now change schools again. Jeanie had turned four without my being at her party. And who knew what their father had been saying about me.

They came home wild, throwing things, running from me even when all I wanted was to wipe their hands. In the middle of nothing, one of them would suddenly scream, "You're bad!" and, in a nerve-wracking ritual, the two of them would jump up and down and chant it in unison. "You're bad! You're bad!"

But if I went to another room, even to the bathroom, they'd run to go with me. If I sat on the couch, one, then the other, would leave her play, climb up against me and just sit. They'd fall asleep only if I sat in their room, and one or both would be in my bed by morning.

All my energy was sapped by the girls and my convalescence, but after a couple of days, I couldn't postpone the school decision any longer. I had to decide whether to drop out or flunk out.

I'd been to only three sessions of each course. With class participation counting for half the grade, that alone meant I couldn't pass the term. Advice from doctors, professors, friends, and advisors was unanimous: Forfeit this first semester, take a leave of absence, fully recuperate, then come back, start the second year over again, and finish my degree.

I ached to take their advice, and if I'd had money and a collaborative ex-husband, I might have. But I had neither, and a leave was impossible. If I left school, I'd lose my student apartment, my financing, and my health insurance. I'd have no degree but all my school debt. It was 1980, and a recession was looming. What job could I get, in that market, with my body still healing and my energy dried up?

I decided my only option was to stay, finish the semester now, and take my chances with the Administrative Board when I inevitably flunked out—or, as we students called it, when I "hit the screen," a bit of slang that conjured up images of my splayed body splatted against a window.

"You do understand," said Worth, "that normal people wouldn't do this, right?"

"So, normal people would choose being homeless and losing their kids?"

She exhaled hard. "Call if you need me. I can get there in sixteen hours if I drive straight through."

Once I hit the screen, I'd have to appeal to the Ad Board for permission to stay on. First, I'd need to demonstrate that I'd flunked out because of extraordinary extenuating circumstances. Traction. Surgery. I figured I had extenuating circumstances covered. But I'd also have to convince the board that I'd be able to complete my degree on time—in other words, successfully complete the final term while also making up the work I'd missed in the first, taking care of the girls, going to physical therapy, finding a job for after graduation, and, if I knew Peter, appearing regularly in court. I myself didn't think I could pull this off.

Still, just going through the appeal process would take me through January and give me another month to recuperate and think about what to do next. And if somehow the Ad Board granted my appeal, I'd be able to stay through June. Worst case, even if I hit the screen in June and didn't get my degree, I'd have had that much more time to pull myself together.

Now that I'd made my decision, I had three weeks to write five papers, take four exams, and flunk out in a way that demonstrated likelihood of success.

We wouldn't get our grades until after the start of the next term, and so I began the second semester with everyone else. In that interlude between finishing exams and getting my grades, I was unnaturally calm. I went to classes and thought little about what lay ahead. My girls began to be themselves again, and we settled into a routine that included a new after-school game called "Doing PT," in which they joined me on the rug and copied my physical therapy exercises in their fashion. Enlisting them to join me kept me disciplined about my therapy, and it was paying off. I'd reached the point where I could open most doors.

Grade day. Students stream to Baker 20, the distribution center where our usual purpose is to pick up new cases for upcoming classes. The room is packed, loud, and haywire with a hundred students' anticipations.

Undistracted by the charge in the air, the "Baker 20 ladies" go about their business. Name? Pull an envelope. Name? Pull an envelope. Some of those stalwart women had seen three generations of outstretched hands go by.

My hand is not outstretched. Until now, I've been in a cocoon that's kept out thoughts of everything this moment will trigger, and I'm not ready to leave it.

"Go on ahead," I say to the person behind me, and to the next, and the next.

Nearly everyone knows my story. A few point me out to their friends, discreetly, they think, but I see them. Several smile. Someone whispers, "Hang in there," as she walks past me to the counter.

Then, somehow, I have an open envelope and a sheet of paper in my hands. Other students veer around me while I stand rooted like a tree in the middle of a sidewalk. I try to read a simple list of course names and the grade in each. But it's the damnedest thing: the letters won't form words.

Suddenly the room goes quiet, and I look up. A large circle has formed, and I'm alone in the center. My friend Richard steps out of the crowd and comes next to me. He takes the letter from my hand and puts his arm around my waist. Whatever the news, I won't fall.

He takes a quick glance at my list. "She made it!" he shouts.

There's cheering and whistling. A Baker 20 lady says, "Hot damn!" and drums the counter with her palms. People move in close, grabbing my arms, reaching out to hug me. A voice hollers, "She just had surgery! Be careful of her back!"

"Thank you. Thank you so much. Thank you." I speak automatically while I try to take it all in. There will be no appeal, no Administrative Board, no having to make up the first semester.

Some said I'd demonstrated a universal truth: You can do anything if you just work hard enough. I think I can, I think I can.

This is pure fiction. I was a decent student in business school, but not a star. And the emphasis on class participation was taken seriously. In real life, the theory went, managers must evaluate options, decide what to do, and convince others to accept their chosen path. The HBS classroom was where we developed and demonstrated these skills. Professors made careful note of our progress, and I'd barely shown up.

So how to make sense of that semester working out? Clearly there'd been clemency in the grading and also abounding luck, both of which were beyond my control and even my imagination.

If I'd flunked the semester and lost my appeal, or won the appeal but crumbled in the final term, people would have called me foolish. As it was, they called me brave, something I never felt. All I'd felt was cornered. I'd been certain I'd flunk out, and, unlikely and convoluted though it was, I'd finally puzzled out a way that staying through that first semester and failing just might work out. I never could see a way that taking a leave might.

At business school I discovered competencies, acquired knowledge and polish, and became self-reliant. But the difficulty of those years left a mark. Going to HBS alone with two young children, little support, and a vengeful ex-husband was a rash gamble that I hadn't thought through. It wouldn't be the last risk I'd ever take, but it would be the last big one I'd take without contemplating the worst that might happen and whether I could deal with it.

I like to think I'm spontaneous, but I'm not. I'd love to have the exuberance of a free spirit, but my internal watchdog sleeps too lightly. That, I suspect, is a legacy of the Harvard days.

As the crowd in Baker 20 thinned out, I worked my way to the exit and went straight to HBS Health Services. The whole staff knew me, and they knew it was grade day. When the receptionist saw my stunned face, she said, "Oh, Marsha," then trailed off and whispered, "I'll get him. Just wait here."

Dr. Kaden left a patient to come see me. Silently, I handed him my letter and watched him read it in the crowded waiting room. "Well," he said quietly, handing it back to me, "that just goes to prove, give people enough rope and sometimes they tie it up neatly."

I left Dr. Kaden and picked up my girls early. We went out to dinner, a rare treat, and that night I slept long and deep. The next morning I would go to classes like every other student. I didn't feel triumphant or even proud, but I got rest and a light at the end of the tunnel, and those were enough.

– 14 –

THE LAUNCH

BETWEEN MASSACHUSETTS LAW REQUIRING ME to have Peter's permission to take the girls out of state and my own refusal to take a job requiring business travel, my job search was limited to a few local employers. The list was precariously short and mostly electronics manufacturers. Not that I was interested in electronics—I wasn't in the least—but in the 1980s, that's where Boston's no-travel senior positions were. Pat, a close friend from business school, suggested I network with Charlie, a fellow alum who was now a manager at Teradyne, one of my target companies.

Charlie and I clicked instantly. Shortly into our conversation he said, "You know, I think Jay, our division head, would like you." Jay was an HBS grad himself, and Charlie promised to put in a good word for me. Wow, I thought. This is going great.

As we were wrapping up, Charlie said again, "I really do think Jay would like you. Let's see if he's in his office," and off he went, out of his office and down a long corridor of cubicles, leaving me no choice but to follow. We turned a corner just in time to see a man hurrying down the hall in the same direction we were going. He had a bit of a limp—bum knee, I thought—which exaggerated his gait and made him seem all the more determined to get where he was going.

"There he is," said Charlie, and that's how it was that the first thing I ever saw of Jay was his back, rushing away. I wanted to stop the pursuit, but Charlie was hell-bent on catching him for my benefit. Some benefit, I thought. He's in a hurry, and now I'm going to delay him. This was no way to impress a potential employer.

"Jay! Hold up!" yelled Charlie.

There was no exaggerated sigh, no conspicuous raise of wrist and pointed glance at watch. Jay just turned, took in Charlie and me coming toward him, leaned casually against a door frame, and waited for us with a smile that filled the building. In a delectable, vaguely British accent I couldn't quite place, he said, "I've got a meeting, but let's talk for a minute or two."

That smile, and the openness and calm of him, immediately put me at ease. I'd assumed that, like all the other executives I'd networked with, he'd ask the usual questions couched in bonhomie but designed to assess my breadth of experience and interest in electronic equipment, but Jay did no such thing.

What a lovely conversation, I thought on my way home, and when I replayed it in my mind, I was startled by how ordinary it had been, and how brief. We'd talked for barely five minutes, at the end of which he knew about my work in Japan, my divorce, and my girls, and I knew I wanted to work at Teradyne.

In spring the campus erupted in flowers, trees greened up, and students in jeans bloomed into professionals in suits. I looked at myself all tricked out and thought, Look at that! I'm the real thing! Flocks of company recruiters descended on the campus every day, and we students signed up for the interviews we wanted.

Preparing for them was serious business. I dutifully studied annual reports and competitive advantages, but I struggled the whole time to keep up my enthusiasm. The hearty boosterism of the managers I'd met networking at other companies had left me cold. In my heart, my already short list was down to one. Teradyne.

I regretted that I'd told Jay I was a single parent. People were incessantly warning me that potential employers believed women were less committed to work than men were.

"Act like a man," they said. "Don't talk about your family."

Teradyne would be sending four recruiters, and Jay was one of them. My plan had been to sign up for him and this time stick to business, but the recruiters' names weren't on the sign-up sheets, and who would interview me was left to chance. Sometimes, though, the winds are benevolent. Into the interview room sailed Jay, leading with his huge smile.

"Hello again," he said. "It's good to see you. I saw you'd signed up and switched you to my list. Since our chat at the office, I've been thinking about what position to offer you."

Without a pause, as though he hadn't just dropped explosive news on me, he started talking about potential roles in which to start me out. I joined him in the conversation as though we were already colleagues. Soon we were swapping Japan stories and laughing over our two unlikely journeys to HBS, his from South Africa via London, where he'd earned a PhD in chemistry only to discover afterward that he didn't like research; mine from Indiana via Japan and blizzard foolery on the tops of cars.

At the end of our meeting, Jay told me I'd be getting an offer in the mail from Teradyne, and even though I had no idea what the salary, benefits, or even my specific job would be, I violated the first rule of negotiation and told him I'd accept. Even today I can see his smile when we shook hands, and I know mine was bright too. It was still on my face when I went to pick up the girls.

"You look happy, Mommy," said Ellen.

In May I handed my last blue book to the exam room proctor and walked outside, a woman transformed. I was no longer a typist, a student, or broke. In just four weeks I'd be making an unimaginable $36,000. The girls and I must celebrate! We must have delicacies! And culture! I mailed off a check for second-balcony season tickets to the ballet for the three of us, bought a whole bag of red peppers at the exorbitant price of sixty-nine cents a pound, and took the girls to dinner at a restaurant with tablecloths.

That we had to vacate our student apartment in four weeks and still had nowhere to go was a matter that would wait until morning.

I'd started my apartment search way back in February—plenty early, had there not been a crackdown on lead paint. Laws about it had been on the books for years but had rarely been enforced. I hadn't even known they existed. Now, landlords who hadn't gone through an expensive lead removal certification process were being assessed large fines if they rented to families with children under five, and Jeanie was four months shy.

For the next two weeks, I dropped the kids off in the morning and looked at apartments until it was time to pick them up. I saw some I liked, but the landlords wanted to see my girls' birth certificates and were unmoved by my pleading that in just four months, three by the time we'd move in, Jeanie would be legal.

One day, my last stop was a place in the nearby suburb of Newton, my first choice because of the excellent school system. The apartment was the entire first floor of a two-family house. It had three large bedrooms, a back porch, and even a butler's pantry. Such beautiful space, I thought, even though all the walls were marred by wide, black tire marks whose origin I couldn't imagine and a wall in one of the bedrooms sported an eight-foot mushroom painted in psychedelic colors.

"Will it be repainted?" I asked, but Anne, the owner, was firm. The apartment would be rented as-is. Well, so what? I loved the apartment and the location, and she hadn't brought up the lead paint laws. I'd repaint on my own, with pleasure.

Anne wasn't a real estate pro. She owned just this house and lived upstairs with her husband, who was deeply lost in dementia. What mattered to her was having a "nice neighbor" downstairs. She hugged me when I said I'd take the apartment and led me upstairs to her kitchen to celebrate with coffee and homemade cookies.

"Look at those curls!" she said over pictures of my girls.

"Your granddaughter looks just like you!" I said, holding a photo of an attractive young woman.

"And your husband?" Anne asked. "Does he work downtown too?"

"It'll be just the girls and me," I said.

She put down the coffee pot and folded her hands in her lap.

"I'm sorry," she said, "but I can't have another divorced woman here. I promised our son."

The previous tenant had been a divorcée and addicted to drugs. Her boys rode their bikes in the house and crashed them into the walls. Men came and went around the clock.

"She cursed at my husband," Anne said, "and the day they moved out, she stuffed the kitchen curtains down the toilet. You can't imagine what the repairs cost. Another divorcée is out of the question."

"How horrible for you," I managed.

I put down my cup and started to leave, but on unchecked impulse I said, "I don't know if this matters, but I'm not divorced. I'm a widow." A few moments later, I'd signed the lease and written her a check.

Back in my car, I started to shake. Peter would be coming and going with the kids, and it wouldn't take Anne long to know that I'd lied.

On June 5, 1980, twenty-two-year-old Caroline Kennedy, daughter of the late President Jack Kennedy, got her Harvard diploma to the flashing of many cameras. Over at the business school, at about the same time, I got mine to the flash of just one. The photo lit by that flash captured everything I cared about that day. I'm in my cap and gown, holding my diploma close to my chest and smiling down at my daughters, who stand with me on the stage. The dean is facing me. His back is to the camera, so there's no way to tell that he's speaking.

"Oh, this is wonderful! Wonderful!" he's saying, as he too looks down at my girls.

A stage and hundreds of chairs had been set out on the lawn. Graduates sat in alphabetical order in the front rows, with family and friends in the rows behind. Somewhere in the crowd, Joyce had my girls. When she saw my row stand to line up by the steps to the stage, she grabbed their hands, ran them down the center aisle, and sat them on the grass in front of the first row. Crouching next to them, she pointed to where I was standing, and they grinned and waved.

The line moved quickly. Up on the stage, grads paused only a few seconds to get their diplomas from the dean and smile at the camera for a single shot. My foot was on the second step when I stopped, turned, and stretched out both hands to Ellen and Jeanie.

"Come with me, girls," I called. "We did this together. Let's finish it together!"

They ran to me in their pretty summer dresses, and we walked hand in hand to center stage. The crowd roared, and the camera clicked.

Probably hundreds of children have crossed that stage by now. I was told I started the tradition. When they saw what I'd done, several of my classmates, all men, broke ranks, ran to their wives, and scooped up infants. They got their diplomas with their babes in their arms, and the crowd cheered every time.

I also cheered, but I couldn't help thinking that they should have taken their wives on stage too.

The day I moved out of student housing, the girls had already left for a month with Peter. The plan was that while they were gone, I'd set up the new apartment and get started at Teradyne. They were excited about having their very own bedrooms when they got back, and I didn't let on that by the end of the summer we might instead be sharing a motel room.

When I arrived with the movers, Anne was waiting in the driveway. She took both my hands in hers and made me promise to call if I needed anything. I smiled weakly. All day I was so preoccupied by the thought that I'd soon be turned out, I unpacked boxes without paying attention to what I was doing. By midafternoon, I needed a rest but couldn't even make myself a cup of coffee. I phoned upstairs.

"Hi, Anne. I need a break, but I can't find my coffee pot. Do you possibly have any instant? I have a cup." Moments later, I was upstairs at her table, drinking her good, brewed coffee.

"I love that you called," she said. "I'm so glad you felt you could," and she started making me a sandwich.

I didn't know a better way to say it, so I just blurted out, "I'm not widowed. I'm divorced."

"I know," she said, slicing a roll. "I've known since the day we signed the lease."

Five miles away lived a woman named Charlotte. She was a close friend of Anne's, and, by pure happenstance, she lived next door to Peter's parents. I'd actually met her a few times.

"I told her what a nice neighbor I'd found," Anne said. "A young widow who went to business school with two little girls and had a good job downtown. Well, Charlotte started hollering, 'She's no widow! She ran out on her husband! His people live right next door!'"

Anne calmly put the sandwich in front of me and poured herself some coffee.

"I yelled right back at her," she said. "'Charlotte,' I told her, 'don't you dare say anything against my neighbor! If you have to be mad at someone, you be mad at me. I forced her to lie!'"

She reached over and patted my hand. "I sat right here and talked to you," she told me. "I could tell you're a good person, and look what I put you through. My son was crazy to make a rule about divorcées, and I was crazier to go along with it."

Anne was my dear friend to the last day of her life. Our only disagreement was over who owed the other an apology for the widow lie. For the five years that we lived there, the girls and I loved every single thing about that house. We still talk about the times we ate watermelon on the back porch and spit the seeds into the grass, the summer night I cancelled bedtime in the middle of reading their goodnight story and, with the girls in sandals and pajamas, we held hands and ran down the hill to the movie theater to see *Snow White*. What the girls couldn't have known was the contentment I felt every time the furnace kicked on, grateful that on my own I could afford to keep us warm. During our time there, Peter would keep acting up, my job would sometimes be rocky, and I'd have another health crisis, but through it all, in that apartment I felt safely harbored.

Teradyne was hiring me for my potential, banking that down the road I'd become a senior executive. As part of my grooming for advancement, I was to be rotated through different positions, and my first job was supervising an assembly department.

It was one of several departments making subassemblies that ultimately went into mainframe-size electronic testing equipment. Twenty assemblers sat at two long worktables, each person doing a highly specialized task. Imagine gravy boats, platters, and tureens instead of soldering guns, cables, and hex keys, and the scene would look like a family Thanksgiving, with items passed from person to person and conversation about kids, politics, and the Red Sox flowing easily.

And if too much heat built up between the young human rights activist working on power supplies and the gruff old conservative doing subassembly button-up, the group leader, Lil Little, kept the sparks from flying. With an exquisite mix of technical knowledge and a feel for when to be tender, stern, wise, or naive, Lil kept the line flowing smoothly. She'd been with Teradyne since the beginning, when the whole company fit around one table, and she knew everyone who'd come on since. The executives valued her and recognized that she had her finger on company pulses they couldn't detect, and she enjoyed an easy familiarity with them.

It was a godsend that Lil kept things going in my department, because I was struggling. Marketing wanted me to agree to finish an assembly ahead of schedule. Engineering wanted confirmation that we could handle a design change. My desk was piled with dozens of change requests like these, and my signoffs were taking days when they should have taken hours.

To make good decisions, I needed what everyone else already had: a detailed knowledge of hundreds of piece parts and components. I was so focused on getting up to speed that summer that when a heat wave in the central US took 1,700 lives, the news managed to escape my notice. Before I fell asleep each night, I drilled myself on printouts of parts with names like H2104-15 and J1240-04, but come morning, I couldn't remember which was which.

It wasn't long before someone complained to my boss— Gene, a dour sort—that I was holding things up. Gene, who reported to Jay, snapped at the guy to stop complaining and give me a hand. Privately, however, he warned me to get up to speed fast. I started taking all the change requests I received to Lil and having her tell me whether to approve them. In this way, I got rid of my sign-off backlog and started my education about what really drove manufacturing.

Soon I was carrying around half-inch-thick accordion-fold printouts with lists of piece parts, covered with handwritten annotations and yellow highlighter. They were awkward and eager as Slinkies to unfurl in my hands and spill all over the floor. Though it was a graceless solution in a culture where street cred came from knowing these things by heart, at least with the printouts in hand I wasn't the sand in the gears anymore.

The girls were scheduled to spend the first half of their winter vacation at Peter's, where his mother, Blanche, would care for them while he was working. For the first time, they balked at going and went off pleading with me to phone them every day. I kept calling, but neither Peter nor Blanche would let me speak with them. The thought that the girls were feeling I'd forgotten them tormented me, and on the spur of the moment I decided to go to New York to visit Minnie and try to take my mind off the situation.

"Blanche and I always got along," Minnie said. "I'll call her."

"Blanche, it's Minnie," I heard her say. "How are you? I feel bad that we haven't been in touch since the kids' divorce."

After some normal niceties, my grandmother said, "The girls are with you? Blanche, I haven't spoken to them in so long. May I say a quick hello?"

Suddenly my grandmother was talking to my daughters, telling them a funny story about a squirrel she'd seen on the sidewalk that morning. After less than a minute, she said, "Your mother's here, and she wants to talk to you," and handed me the receiver.

The girls and I talked for a few happy moments. I just had time to say, "I'm picking you up the day after tomorrow," before Blanche grabbed the phone from them and hung up.

"That's that between Blanche and me," said Minnie, "but the girls needed to hear your voice."

When I got back to work, Lil came into my office. "We always get people in here from Harvard, MIT, places like that," she said. "They come in high and mighty, think they'll turn this department into the gem of the ocean and be some kind of hero." On top of all my other shortcomings, I'd apparently been high and mighty.

"I've been watching you," she said. "I like you. I'm going to help you."

I still had no idea what problem I'd created. "Help me with what?"

Lil laughed. "I don't know, but some time or other everybody needs help."

She must have been clairvoyant. Two weeks later, no assembler met my eyes when I got in. "Good morning!" I called out, but only a thin mumble rose in response. Then I saw a note on my desk, written in thick black marker on a large piece of cardboard torn from a shipping carton. "See Gene at once!" Next to it was a long newspaper article. Cut not from some obscure rag but from the *Boston Globe*, it was a supposed profile of me, written in Q&A format complete with harebrained quotes I'd never uttered. I knew nothing about the article and had never met the reporter.

". . . fastest typist in the East . . . didn't really want to be a typist . . . Harvard MBA is a guarantee . . ." It made me sound like an entitled dingbat.

My consulting in Japan wasn't mentioned, but the fact that I'd missed a whole semester of business school because of my back injury was highlighted. Worst of all, my salary was disclosed. "Her Job Lacked Challenge, So She Got a Harvard Degree" was the headline. It might as well have been "She Got into Harvard with No Qualifications and Makes More Money Than You Do."

Gene's hard voice hit me like a fist. "What were you thinking?" His nostrils flared when I pleaded innocence.

From Gene's office I went straight to Jay's. "I'm so sorry," I said. "It makes you look bad for hiring me, and people will resent my salary."

"Oh, I'm always being second-guessed," he said. "One time more or less won't matter, and everyone knows we pay more for advanced degrees." His eyes were kind. "Don't worry. This will pass."

Lil was waiting in my office when I got downstairs. "You saw Gene? Did you go see Jay? Good. Now you just stay cool," she told me. "Just go about your business. You got people here watching your back."

She nodded through the glass wall of my office to the assembly workers. Most were now looking up at me, several smiling with encouragement. Two waved. I knew she'd already started the hard work of changing the office drumbeat.

It took only a day to track down the source of the article. A woman whose nonprofit had given me financial aid for my MBA had wanted the paper to profile her organization, and she'd used my story to illustrate their good work. Only when the article came out did she discover that the reporter had turned me into the headliner.

She was philosophical about it. Her agency was prominent in the piece, and she was mentioned by name. My own reaction mystified her. "Mortified?" she asked. "Why aren't you proud?"

When I complained to the *Boston Globe* for running the fake interview, I got nowhere, and since there was no real remedy they could offer, I decided not to push it. For a while, I felt bumbly whenever I met someone new at Teradyne. I was sure they were thinking, "Oh, she's the overpaid typist." But Jay was pretty much right. The newspaper piece hung in the air for a bit and then blew over, at least overtly.

Despite my ineptitudes and the article, I did have friends at work. When one of our group, an unmarried executive, finally managed to buy a house, we all took her out to celebrate. Despite her long tenure and executive position, it had taken her a year to find a bank that would give her a mortgage without a male relative's co-signature.

There were even some men in my life. I went out with one of the salesmen briefly before dating an engineer who was smart, funny, and adorable. One night, he joined the girls and me for dinner. At the table, I pulled over Ellen's plate to cut up her chicken, then Jeanie's, and then, my mind elsewhere, I pulled over the engineer's plate and started cutting his chicken too. I pulled myself together only when the girls started laughing.

I'd learned that afternoon that I was pregnant.

Saying nothing to the cute engineer, I had a D&C and talked at length with my gynecologist about having my tubes tied. I decided to have the procedure and scheduled it for a few months out, when my daughters would be at Peter's for a week.

Several days later, the girls and I were at the ballet when a pain in my shoulder started up. Soon it was so severe I couldn't sit still. Finally, unable to bear it, I whispered to Ellen and Jeanie that we had to leave and slid out of my seat and toward the exit before they could protest.

When we got home, I heard the phone ringing through the back door, but I was foggy-brained and fumbled with my keys. Once I got the door open, I had trouble focusing and zigzagged back and forth across the kitchen before the receiver was in my hand. It was my gynecologist calling.

"I couldn't answer the phone," I said. "My shoulder hurts."

He screamed at me to pay attention, yelled that I should call 911, ordered me to meet him at the hospital right away.

"Do you understand? Can you do that?"

I said yes, but instead of 911, I called friends. Then I went into shock and slid down the wall to the floor.

"The lab found no sign of pregnancy in the tissue samples!" is what he'd been yelling. "Your pregnancy is ectopic! It's in a fallopian tube, not your uterus! I think it's ruptured! This can kill you!" I'd been hemorrhaging into my abdomen without symptoms until enough blood accumulated to provoke the nerve that sent ice picks into my shoulder.

Ellen was eight and Jeanie, six. They could easily unlock and open the front door, but I'd taught them not to unless I was right there with them. Fortunately, they thought for themselves that day and opened it when our friends arrived. On the way to the hospital, I was in and out of consciousness and mostly out of sense. I'm told that along with a bunch of gibberish I kept repeating, "Take the girls. I'll call you soon."

A medical team was waiting for us in the parking lot. Two nurses sprinted down the hall on either side of my flying stretcher, prepping me on the way to the operating room. At one point my gynecologist's voice penetrated. "You've lost a fallopian tube. Do you want me to tie the other one? You have to sign. Can you sign?" A pen was slipped into my hand and a clipboard thumped onto my chest. I made some kind of mark.

My surgery took more than six hours. The beckoning light that many report didn't shine for me, nor did I have a vision of myself floating above the operating room, but I was told I died on the table from severe hemorrhaging and was then revived. My hospital stay was long because of widespread infection and a blood clot in my calf, the result of the long surgery. I told everyone, including the cute engineer, that I'd had a ruptured ovarian cyst, a nice, chaste catastrophe.

One afternoon, Jay visited me in the hospital with his wife, Lydia, whom I hadn't yet met. She wore plain khaki slacks and an unremarkable white shirt, and her voice was appropriately muted for the setting. Yet something about her burst like a marching band through the hospital banality of beeping machines and time-erasing routine. Full of stitches and infection, I was no match for her vigor, and I felt grateful to my hospital gown and the tubes in my arm for absolving me from keeping up my end of a conversation.

When Jay stepped out to find a payphone, Lydia scooted her chair closer to my bed and stage-whispered, "I know about Japan, your divorce, your kids, your whole story. I have my own file on you, but Jay doesn't know."

I just looked at her, unable to follow the thread. It turned out that Lydia was on the Combined Jewish Philanthropies scholarship board, the board that had lent me the final $1,500 I'd needed for business school.

"Jay came home one day and said he'd just met a terrific woman who'd lived in Japan and gone to HBS alone with two little girls. I knew it had to be you," she said. "Of course, I couldn't say anything because of the board's confidentiality rules. He said he wanted to hire you, and I didn't even look up. I just said, 'That's nice,' and kept washing the lettuce."

A few years later, I would join that scholarship board myself and learn what she'd neglected to tell me: that she'd single-handedly gotten me my award. By policy, the board didn't cover living expenses for dependents, and they'd disqualified me when they saw that my shortfall was because of the girls' expenses. Lydia, like all the others, had accepted that policy for years, but something snapped when she saw my application. She wanted an amendment, and she fought for it.

"Like a tiger!" a committee member told me. "She said we were behind the times and just kept hammering and hammering until we all agreed."

Even though I gave her permission to tell Jay, Lydia wouldn't break confidentiality, so when he came back from his call, I broke it for her. No one could ever have made this up, we kept telling each other. Who could imagine such a coincidence?

Certainly none of us imagined then what that loan had set in motion.

– 15 –

SHAWMUT

BY THE TIME I WAS WELL enough to go back to Teradyne, I'd done some thinking about my job. There was no position higher than mine that I wanted, and the culture didn't appeal to me or play to my strengths. I worked primarily with the old guard, who settled things through combat. The trim, boyish engineering manager looked congenial and fought quietly. He'd stand and listen, looking a little bit bored, and mildly intone, "That doesn't matter," to anything he didn't agree with. The production manager was a beefy guy who hollered and stabbed his cigar at people. Bev, a friend who had a job similar to mine, didn't reach his shoulder even in heels, but she'd plant herself firmly in front of him and stab back. She'd match the engineering manager put-down for put-down and, unfazed and even energized, come back for more the next day. But I was fed up with this stuff.

I'd gotten a promotion, and then another, and along the way I'd discovered a talent for figuring out and fixing the reasons work didn't flow properly. My third anniversary at

Teradyne was approaching. It seemed I had a future there if I wanted it, but I decided the right thing for me was to leave both Teradyne and manufacturing.

The many financial services companies in Boston needed not just people who could grant loans and sell mortgages, but also people who could make backroom processing flow smoothly, a specialty of mine. I networked with a friend, the friend knew a guy, one thing led to another, and I was offered a job running a unit of about a hundred people in the Mutual Funds Division at the Shawmut Bank, now part of Bank of America. It was a very broken unit in a very broken division. A fix-it job, just the kind of thing I liked best.

During my interview, Fred, the new division head who would become my boss, rolled my resume into a tube and absently drummed his desk with it while he looked out the window, thinking things over. We'd been talking about the division's problems for a little over an hour. I'd drawn several analogies between financial transaction processing and manufacturing and had made a big pitch about how relevant my Teradyne experience was. After a minute or two, he turned and looked at me through my rolled-up resume, as though it were a spyglass. "Do you even know what a mutual fund is?" he asked.

"What a mutual fund is?" I repeated. "I do." And I rattled off, "It's a pool of money from individuals or institutions that's invested by professional money managers in stocks, bonds, and other securities." Then I rolled my eyes and fessed up that I'd read that in a library book just the night before.

He tossed my resume into the wastebasket.

"Yeah, I figured," he said. "Look, we're full of mutual fund experts. I need someone with your operations background. I guess you're smart enough to learn what you need to about the funds."

Jay had taken the same gamble when he hired me at Teradyne, and it hadn't paid off. This time, I felt things would be different. Fred's situation was exactly the kind I liked, a complicated problem that had to do with how people, not piece parts, did their jobs and how all the roles worked together.

When I gave my notice at Teradyne, Jay congratulated me and promised lunch after I settled in at Shawmut. His senior team, all but Gene, were also gracious, seasoned enough to know that not all hires work out for the long run. Gene was Gene. He wouldn't look up when I went to tell him my news, and he sulked at my goodbye party.

Shawmut's customers were the mutual fund management companies that owned the funds and made the investment decisions. We were the back room department that processed their shareholders' instructions for them. Shareholder calls came to our phones, and our staff answered with the funds' names.

My unit was responsible for mutual funds belonging to thirty different management companies, and that meant thousands of shareholders, most of them furious. And who wouldn't be? Somehow things had gone very much awry. The division had made profound errors, such as buying or selling shares at the wrong price or putting one person's shares in another's account. Repaying shareholders for losses caused by these errors was costing Shawmut a fortune, and regulatory violations were severe.

The SEC had blocked the division from taking on new customers and had given us a year to get compliant or be shut down. Shawmut's board wanted a return to profitability by the end of the same year and had hired Fred, a rock star in the mutual funds world, to build a new team and turn things around. We all knew the stakes: Miss those conjoined one-year deadlines, and it would be off with our heads.

The casual dresses and skirts I'd worn at Teradyne wouldn't do at Shawmut. Hanging in my closet were strange new clothes that seemed to belong to someone whose shape was very different from mine. Cut from men's suiting, the jackets hung in military formation, man-tailored and disdainful of womanly curves. The shirts were no-nonsense button-down things that needed tiny safety pins between the buttons to prevent gaps and a scandalous flash of bra. They tucked into austere skirts with trivial kick pleats that prevented long strides. Ten years later, senators Barbara Mikulski and Carol Moseley Braun would wear trousers on the senate floor in defiance of the rule that forbade women to do so—audacious when they did it and unthinkable when I was at Shawmut.

I'd been in Japan when the Women's Movement went wide in the US, and after my return I'd been too consumed by Peter's provocations, the girls, and my two medical emergencies to pay it much attention. It didn't occur to me to question why the women were dressed in men's uniforms. The fact is, I loved those unforgivable suits. When I put one on in the morning, I felt sharp and ready for whatever waited at the office.

What waited at the office was chaos. The aisles of the polished, corporately-upholstered division had been taken over by crocodiles of ugly brown tables at which sat scores of temps who double-checked every transaction. Scores more double-checked the double-checking in a ham-handed attempt to prevent new errors while we cleared the backlog of old ones. Frustrated shareholders were bypassing us and taking their grievances directly to the fund management companies, who in turn were threatening to move their funds to our competitors.

For three weeks I observed how staff handled every transaction and handoff, from the moment instructions arrived by mail or phone until processing was completed and the paperwork archived. At night I studied SEC regulations. Then I was on and off airplanes for a month, visiting the fund companies and trying to inspire enough confidence to convince them to give us time to turn things around. In the end, no fund companies pulled out, and by the end of the year the division was both compliant and profitable.

I hadn't been told about the possibility of a bonus, and so I was surprised and elated to receive a special check of $1,100 for retaining all my clients, turning around my operations groups, and landing the first new client when the SEC lifted its restrictions. Along with the money, I got one of Shawmut's "lady ties," a thin strip of blue silk fetchingly adorned with the corporate logo. I saw it as a badge of honor and proudly tied it around my neck, where it hung in a bow as limp and scraggy as yarn on little girls' pigtails.

I can pinpoint the exact moment my feminist consciousness was raised and I plugged into the Women's Movement. It was when I learned that despite my bigger achievements, men I worked with got hugely larger bonuses and no damn bow.

Gone were the tables of temps. The division was prettied up and sold to a competitor. Fred, my boss, and others on the senior team went with it, but I stayed at Shawmut and got a new position consolidating the purchasing and warehousing functions of the thirteen subsidiary banks. I worked hard, and I loved it. I was promoted to vice president.

I bought us a little house, and the girls started fifth and seventh grades in their new schools. Peter never did pay child support, but now I could manage without his money. What I wanted but couldn't make happen was an end to his harassment. One freezing night, when he brought Ellen and Jeanie back, he rang my doorbell, then peeled off their winter coats and ran away with them before I got to the door, leaving the girls stunned and shivering on the porch. He cancelled their health insurance, which I learned only after I took one of them to the doctor and received a large bill. I kept sensing him out there somewhere, armed with grenades he could throw at any moment.

When suddenly he got a new lawyer, I expected an uptick in summonses, but court dates actually got fewer and farther between. Several months later, I got a call from his first lawyer, the teacup guy. Peter hadn't dropped this lawyer, it turned out. The lawyer had dropped him.

"His unpaid legal bills go way back," Teacup said, "and I was wondering, since you've had the same problem with him, do you have any suggestions on how I might collect?"

"Sorry," I said, and I hung up without even adrenalizing.

Over time, those grenades I'd imagined came to feel like peashooters. I saw I was dealing with a man who was unbalanced and angry but not omnipotent. The girls and I had had troubles, and I'd gotten us through them. I'd found my talents, and I could support us. We finally had a manageable life, and Peter's occasional flare-ups felt more bothersome than consequential.

There came a morning when Shawmut officers were told to drop what we were doing and assemble in the auditorium. On the stage were our board chair, our CEO, and some men we didn't recognize. They told us Shawmut and a similar-sized company, Connecticut National Corporation, were merging. Our CEO and the one from Connecticut recounted with relish how they'd negotiated secretly, in unlikely places, throwing off anyone who might be tailing them by entering buildings through one door and leaving through another to jump into different vehicles waiting with engines running. Oh, those lionhearted James Bonds. How fun for them.

Now there were two headquarters, two HR heads, two marketing heads, two heads of IT, public relations, loans. . . . Heads of every department marched two by two into a new world that wanted only one of each. We'd been told this would be a "merger of equals," but the new senior executives were all from Connecticut National. They took over our cafeteria like occupying soldiers. Most Shawmut managers were fired and their departments absorbed by their Connecticut counterparts. We had mournful goodbye parties for our colleagues almost every day, and soon whole floors were empty. What would happen to my department and our Connecticut counterpart hadn't yet been addressed, but we knew our turn would come. Impending unemployment loomed over my staff and me. The whole thing was lousy.

– 16 –

JAY FROM TERADYNE

AFTER TERADYNE, JAY AND I had stayed in touch through occasional lunches. I'd been at Shawmut for five years when I answered my phone at work one day, and a woman I didn't know said, "I believe you knew Lydia."

She kept talking, but my mind was stuck on the stark past-tenseness of "knew."

"Wait," I said. "Lydia died? What happened?"

The woman took a small breath before saying, "She took her own life. Her disorder, you know."

But I didn't know. Lydia had had bipolar disorder, and on a terrible day it had overwhelmed her.

At the funeral, Jay's two sons, in their twenties, and his daughter, about to enter college, entered the sanctuary in a tight cluster. Jay was in the center, bent over as though he couldn't bear the weight of his own bones. Slowly he made his way to the front pew, supported by his children. I caught just one glimpse of his face, so raw and exposed I turned my eyes away, the only thing I could do for him.

Back at his house, at the shiva, Jay was shrunken on the couch. He periodically scanned the room for his children, and when he caught the eye of one, he patted the seat next to him and the son or daughter would go sit with him, both of them looking out of reach and fragile. I tried to understand what they were feeling, but it was impossible. I hadn't yet felt grief like that, the kind that makes you feel sheathed in glass and tuned to shatter.

For months after the funeral, I thought of him but didn't call. Seeing his naked grief had felt too intimate, and I didn't know what to say. Even though my fat teenage self with doomed crushes on unattainable boys was twenty-five years in the past, when Jay became single I felt like that girl again, painfully self-conscious despite having known him for eight years and afraid that proposing lunch might sound like I was asking him on a date. My imagination turned us into two people we weren't: an awkward adolescent and an unapproachable man.

It was easy to let time go by. The girls had their school activities, friends, and, recently on the scene, boyfriends. I'd started teaching a management course in Boston University's MBA program, and at Shawmut I was caught up in office indignities. A year had passed since the merger, and no Shawmut department head had prevailed in the consolidation. Now it was my department's turn to be pitted against its Connecticut counterpart to see which would survive. My senior staff and I had every expectation that we would soon be gone.

The Consolidation Committee was insatiable for data about our activity, and to insulate my staff from having to feed the monster that wanted to eat us, I pulled much of it together myself. Several nights a week I worked until nine or ten, and I was at the office most weekends.

One Sunday morning, I got there around 8:00 and found on my desk a large manila envelope that hadn't been there when I'd left at 11:00 the night before. *Confidential* was scrawled across it in thick black marker, and it was sealed with a preposterous amount of tape. Inside was a copy of a report laying out the results of the Consolidation Committee's work. Sure enough, my department was being eliminated.

I'd expected this, but seeing it in black and white made me sick to my stomach. For several minutes I sat with my head in my hands and my eyes closed, and then a single phrase from the report surfaced in my mind and sounded an alarm. When I started reading again, I realized that all the Shawmut data was false. The real numbers would have kicked Connecticut out of contention.

I sat back hard in my chair. I had a notion of who'd left this for me, and as though this were a B movie, my suspect entered the scene at that very moment. A Consolidation Committee member from Connecticut crept into the darkened department, then, clearly shocked to see the lights on in my office and me at my desk, froze in the doorway.

"You may as well come all the way in," I called.

The poor man was haggard, his face stubbly. He wouldn't acknowledge that he'd left me the report, but he disclosed that when the committee reported to the Connecticut higher-ups that our department had superior results in all categories, they were instructed to write a new report and conclude the opposite.

My heart went out to him. He'd spent weeks in Boston interviewing my staff and me and going through our files, and I'd come to know him as a good guy. A loyal employee and man of integrity, working for the victor but unable to make peace with its tactics, he must have agonized over the bogus report, agonized about leaving it for me, and agonized through the night before deciding to come retrieve it. Now he was caught.

"I won't tell anyone we spoke about this," I said. "Please thank whoever left it for me," and I put the report in my desk and locked the drawer.

The next morning I took it to my boss, along with the correct graphs and tables that had originally been given to the committee.

"Good girl," he said, when I declined to reveal my source.

He and I never mentioned the leaked report again. I don't know how he managed it, but soon it was announced that Massachusetts and Connecticut purchasing, warehousing, and distribution would be merged under my leadership and headquartered in Boston. My staff and I were proud but mostly relieved. Now we had bigger jobs, and, more importantly, a better story to tell prospective employers than if we'd been laid off. Almost all of us still wanted out.

Doing a job search was tricky. Two days a week my senior managers and I commuted to Hartford, where a suspicious, resentful staff now reported to us. In Massachusetts, rumors circulated that any Shawmut employees caught job-hunting were immediately let go under the guise of consolidation. We didn't totally believe it, but we weren't taking any chances.

It took me a year to find a new position. Fred, my old boss in the mutual funds division, was now a very senior executive at Fidelity Investments, and he recommended me for a position there. By sheer luck, the man who would become my new manager worked in a Fidelity building right across the street from Shawmut headquarters. For interviews, I could leave my office carrying a manila folder and a notebook, with no coat or bag, looking as though I were going to a meeting in our building.

When I started my new job at Fidelity, I felt excited about work for the first time in the two years since Shawmut had been taken over. I was the vice president overseeing the internal auditors who perpetually examined Fidelity's divisions for accuracy and regulatory compliance.

Though auditing didn't particularly excite me, the job also involved creating a new internal consulting department, which would be enough fun to more than compensate. Fidelity was legendary for encouraging employees to move around into different roles to broaden their knowledge of the company and maximize their talents. Common wisdom said to take any job just to get in and then, from the inside, find a way to move to a better slot. I hoped this was true, but regardless, I would have crawled on my hands and knees to get that position, so seductive were the energy and industriousness I'd felt at Fidelity compared to the gloom pervading Shawmut.

One evening, Jay and I bumped into each other in a supermarket, and when our small talk started turning into a full-blown conversation, we pulled out our calendars to set a time to get together. He now worked in Teradyne's New Hampshire subsidiary, so lunch wouldn't work. We settled on dinner the following week at Cafe Freesia, a local restaurant convenient to both our commutes.

I arrived first. Time passed, and I checked my lipstick. As more time passed, I figured he was stuck in New Hampshire traffic. It got later, and I was sure he'd forgotten our dinner and gone straight home. But then there he was, just inside the door, scanning the restaurant for me.

With his light complexion, light hair, and light blue eyes, he seemed to radiate light himself, and something in me leaned his way. We talked happily and stayed long enough at dinner for other tables to empty of diners and fill again.

Ellen, then sixteen, got home from her evening out right after I pulled in from mine.

"How was your date?" she asked.

"It wasn't a date," I said. "It was Jay, from Teradyne. We had a nice time. He was a little late, but once he got there it was fine."

"Are you interested in him?" she asked.

"Don't be silly," I said. "It's just Jay. From Teradyne. Remember him?"

"Were you worried when he was late?

"Of course not. My plan was to come home if he wasn't there by 6:30, but he was."

"How late was he?" she asked.

"It was nothing. Just seven or eight minutes."

"Eight minutes late and you already had a plan? Don't tell *me* you're not interested!"

Over the next year, Jay and I slowly reconnected—calls here and there, an occasional meal. One day I phoned his office, and the Teradyne operator said, "He no longer works here."

"Is he back at the Boston office?" I asked.

"He's no longer with the company."

I reached him at home. He'd been laid off the previous day and would be going to New Hampshire that Sunday to clear out his office.

"Who's going with you?" I asked.

"No one," he said. "It's just a few boxes."

I seemed to be more upset by his layoff than he was.

"Letting yourself into a deserted building, turning the lights out behind you. It seems like a sad end to all your years there," I said.

We talked for a while about other things, and at the end he said, "You know, I think it would be nice after all if you came with me on Sunday."

When we got there, Jay unlocked the door and hit light switches as we walked the dark corridors, illuminating ahead of us stretches of workstations with the usual hash of papers, coffee cups, photos, and the occasional pair of high heels under a desk. In his office, we readily fell into a congenial rhythm. He sorted through files while I packed the personal items from his desk and bookshelves and wandered the ghostplace to find more wastebaskets. A few laughs over now-irrelevant office drama, some wisecracks about the volume of trash, a search for one more empty box, and suddenly the job was done. Jay put notes on a few people's chairs while I went to dump the cold remains of our vending-machine coffee.

It was dark when we left, and we stopped for pizza. He said he was planning to go to the beach in a couple of weeks and invited me along. Getting ready, I was ridiculous. I packed grapes and peanuts, then took them out of my tote and packed plums and crackers. I put on jeans and switched my shirt three times.

The fall day was cool and overcast, and no one else was on the beach when we spread out our things. Conscious of the clichéd setting and our being together on a blanket, I was mannered and a little stiff. I sat facing the water, with my arms around my knees. Jay lay on his side, his head propped up on his cupped hand, facing me. We talked for a bit, until I said something and got silence in return. Jay had rolled onto his back and was sound asleep.

He slept on, and I went from amused to bored to annoyed. Date-gone-bad was a common theme among my single friends. One had recently reported, "He talked all night to a friend he spotted at another table. Afterward he wanted to split the bill because we hadn't really spent the time together."

Just what I wanted, I thought. Another entry in the catalog of bad dates. Immediately I was ashamed of myself. Jay wasn't some blind date. He was a good man, a friend for eleven years. Two years earlier he'd lost his wife, and now he'd just lost his job. In its stillness, his face seemed to absorb the air and sun and fill out, and I noticed only in its absence the exhaustion that had been there earlier. His magazine was on the blanket next to him, and I slipped it back into his bag so the wind flipping its pages wouldn't wake him.

I read my book to the sound of the ocean and the calm of Jay's deep sleep. After a while, the sun moved past the visor of his cap and onto his eyes, and I swiveled around so my book would throw a shadow on his face. In that direction, I saw a lanky teenager and his dog splashing along the water's edge two hundred feet down the shore. Suddenly the dog vaulted our way, a big shaggy galumph of a hound with his teen at his heels, shouting and making wild grabs at the trailing leash. They were on us before I could react.

The dog leaped and landed with his two front paws right on Jay's chest. Jay woke with a gasp, worked himself into a sitting position, and held both sides of the dog's face, saying, "Good boy. Good boy." The owner ran for Jay's hat, blown into nearby scrub, then came back and grabbed the leash. Flinging flustered apologies over his shoulder, he dragged the unwilling dog up the shore as we tried to stifle our laughs.

Jay came over for dinner the next night, and we worked together on his resume. It turned out we were excellent collaborators. He started calling to debrief me after each of his interviews, and together we talked through what his next steps might be. We celebrated when he got the job offer he wanted, and then we strategized his contract negotiations together.

By the time he started his new position, our lives had begun to intertwine. Typically, we met for dinner one night during the week, and we had a Sunday routine of an afternoon movie or theater matinee, after which we stopped by his house to walk Shaka, his beautiful golden retriever/German shepherd mix, and then went out to dinner. Strolling through Jay's quiet neighborhood, we made a pleasing picture of peaceful domesticity—man, woman, dog. Maybe one day, I thought.

On one of our weeknight dinners, a very heavy woman walked by our table. For the first time in a few years, I felt the old sensation of not having a sense of my own size. "Am I the same size as her?" I wondered, and at Jay's reaction, I realized I'd asked it out loud. He laughed awkwardly. I met his eyes and shrugged, embarrassed. Jay stopped laughing and answered as though I'd just asked something normal. "There's no comparison," he said. "You're slim."

More than twenty years earlier, I'd held cookies by my face to hide a diet. Now, so long afterward, I'd once more lost my sense of my own body. In the years to come, I would gain and lose weight again, but this would be the last time I'd lose touch with my size. I looked down at my legs and saw a flat lap. Seeing myself through the eyes of someone I trusted, I understood that the large belly I'd felt resting on my thighs had been a phantom limb.

Jay called often to say goodnight, and I, an executive who sat on boards, taught graduate students, and was invited to speak at conferences, became an infatuated teenager. If the phone rang in the evening, I ran for it, yelling to the girls, "I've got it!" I channeled Stevie Wonder and sang in the shower, *"I just called to say I love you."*

"You're in love," said Marina. She was standing at her front door, watching me walk up from my car. She and Michael had come a long way since arriving bootless in Boston in a blizzard. They had a house not far from mine, where we often talked until midnight over Marina's fine Russian cooking. "You've met someone," she said. "You look completely different. I can see it all over you."

"It's this dress," I said. "It's new."

"The dress is nice, but I know what I see."

One afternoon, Jay called from the airport.

"Where are you off to?" I asked.

"Visiting some friends on the West Coast," he said. "They're about to call my flight, and I already miss you."

"I miss you too," I said. It was the first time we'd expressed our feelings—a waypost I painted with shimmery significance.

That I'd been unaware of his trip wasn't surprising. Though we saw each other once or twice a week, we still led largely separate lives. So far, we'd gone out just on our own, and after his call from the airport, I decided to nudge us one more step along the way to coupledom—going out together with friends and colleagues. I invited him to a party thrown by my boss at Fidelity.

"Sure!" he said, with his huge smile and no hesitation.

Two young women on my staff openly ogled the handsome, engaging man I'd brought. The next morning, they pounced on me at the office. His sexy accent, how great we looked together—they wanted the scoop. Were Jay and I serious?

Oh yes, I thought, but I wasn't about to offer us up for dissection at the water cooler. "We're old friends," I said. "We worked together a long time ago."

– 17 –

THERE'S A WOMAN

WHEN HE CAME OUT HIS front door, his face WAS glowing the way I knew mine was. He walked toward my car with that hitch in his gait that I always saw as a spring in his step, and when he climbed in, we sat like two dopes for a minute, just grinning at each other.

Then he said, "I have to tell you something."

I turned off the engine and looked at him, my hands in my lap.

"You need to know," he said. "There's a woman."

A voice in my head directed, "Be still. Don't move. Just listen." A part of me left my body and even the car and hovered somewhere high above us, watching my face stay calm as I sat silently.

"Her name's Eve," he said. "She's a friend of the Kramers, and after Lydia died . . ."

Dave and Betty Kramer, Jay's best friends. I'd heard much about the Kramers, but I hadn't met them. And in that instant, I realized two things: that Jay and I had never gone out on a

Saturday, and that all those Saturdays he said he'd hung out with the Kramers, they'd been a foursome.

"I keep telling her I want to break up, but she gets hysterical. You can't imagine. She yells. She throws things." I heard real fear in his voice. "I'm afraid she'll do something."

Do something, I thought, like his late wife got distraught and did something. Even in my shock, I felt compassion. The hovering part of me returned to my body, and the voice in my head said, So you can live with this? This is okay with you?

Jay was saying something about a trip.

". . . and when I called you from the airport that time, it was her friends we were on our way to see."

The glitter I'd put on that phone call drifted to the ground and landed as so much dust.

"I haven't slept with her in . . ." but I was not about to listen to this.

"So, you have a girlfriend," I said, neutrally, I think.

"No, not a girlfriend. I told you. I don't even like her. My kids can't stand her. She . . ."

"Jay, you and Eve see each other every weekend. You get together with friends as a couple. You travel as a couple. That's a girlfriend." I was talking to him, but also to myself, crystallizing my stand on this thing I'd never considered. "I don't go out with men who have girlfriends," I said. "And I won't be some pal you can complain to about Eve." I waited and refused to fill the silence for him.

After a few moments he said, "I'll fix this."

Ask a thousand women, and at least nine hundred will tell you I fell for the oldest line in the book: "I will leave her for you."

The fact is, I did realize Jay might never leave Eve, but I also knew that his glow when we were together was as real as mine, and I decided to take a chance.

"Good," I said, and we went on to a movie, where we'd been going all along.

– 18 –

DOINGS AND UNDOINGS

IDELITY CRACKLED WITH THE VOLTAGE of the mutual fund boom and the ability to put its money where its aspirations were. My auditing staff was crackerjack at evaluating each department's quality control and regulatory compliance, and I augmented their work by identifying ways the departments could improve efficiency and customer service. Meanwhile, I completely missed a drama playing out just beyond my office door.

Before I'd started at Fidelity, my new boss had alerted me that my audit manager, a bright, ambitious guy with street smarts, had wanted my job and resented a non-auditor coming in over him. "If he gets up to any mischief," my boss said, "just let me know."

As months passed, I didn't have any issues with the audit manager, but my boss became a challenge. He'd call me to his office, give me a rambling account of something he'd read in a book or heard on the radio, and then repeat it, verbatim, two or even three times, apparently unaware that he'd just told me the identical story. When he summoned me shortly after his return from a couple of weeks in the London office, I steeled myself for another rambling conversation, but this time he was extremely succinct.

"I'm sure this comes as no surprise," he said. "I'm firing you."

It came as a total surprise. It came as a shot from a stun gun. Before I could respond, he said the audit manager had called him in London to complain about me, and those complaints were why I was being let go. I tried to have a conversation, to suggest less drastic ways we might deal with the situation, but his mind was made up. An announcement would be made in two weeks, and in six weeks I'd be out of work. With that, he waved me away.

Clear thoughts wouldn't come. I tried to reach Jay, was told he was visiting a client, and walked over to a friend's office in the next department. Her position was senior to mine, and when I started to tell her what had just happened, she put a finger to her lips and got up to close her office door.

"The executives are watching your boss," she said quietly. "He's been acting erratically, and they've noticed." One of those noticing, she said, was Nita.

Nita was the president of a large Fidelity subsidiary that, among other things, did the same kind of backroom processing for Fidelity's funds that I'd done at Shawmut for smaller fund companies. She was astute, quick-witted, and extremely approachable. After my staff had audited her organization, I'd shared with her some of my ideas to strengthen her operation, and she'd listened intently. When I called to let her know I'd just been fired, she asked a lot of questions and said I'd hear from her within the week.

"I can't promise anything," she said, "but if you get an offer before I call you back, check in with me before you accept it."

Only a few days later, she offered me the position of vice president of operations, reporting directly to her—a dream job under a dream boss. Shortly thereafter, the man who'd fired me suddenly left Fidelity amid rumors about his health.

In my new position, I oversaw several transaction-processing departments as well as the subsidiary's legal department. I also launched new products and represented Nita's division on committees with the heads of marketing and IT.

My staff, around two hundred people, included a lot of bright young people in their late twenties and early thirties. At any given time, a number of them were buying their first house, getting married, having a baby, or doing two of the three. When women still on maternity leave came in to show off their babies, they often needed a place to nurse in privacy. Those still nursing when they came back from leave needed a place to pump their breasts to provide their sitters and au pairs with bottles of breast milk for the babies.

My departments were in Boston's World Trade Center, at the water end of a low building that ran the entire length of a long pier into the harbor. We had spectacular views, and our area was full of natural light. Most people worked in cubicles separated by low partitions, and drapes were forbidden on the glass walls of private offices on the building's perimeter so that the views and light could be enjoyed by as many employees as possible.

In one of my areas, I had a vacant interior office with neither views nor natural light. I decided to try pulling rank. Pretending not to notice the winces of the maintenance manager when I said "breast pump" or "nursing," I ultimately got him to agree to install drapes and put a lock on that office door. There was no official announcement to employees, but word spread. Fidelity's nursing room became a frequently-used, quiet sensation long before "lactation room" was ever uttered in corporate circles.

Ellen had gone off to college, and Jeanie's junior year in high school was wrapping up. One spring weekend she went to visit a friend, and, like always when she was away, I stayed at Jay's. We were in bathrobes at his kitchen table when we heard a key turn in the lock and the front door open. A voice called out, "Honey?" Jay went white and stood up at the same instant a woman entered the kitchen. I knew who it had to be.

"Hello, Eve," I said quietly.

I stayed seated. She ignored me.

"You said you didn't have this kind of relationship with her," she snapped at Jay.

A bathrobe relationship, some slow part of my brain translated, while another, double-time part frenetically called plays like a sportscaster. She doesn't call before she comes. She has a key. She calls him honey. They've talked about me.

Shaka's collar tags clanged against his water bowl. The dishwasher changed cycles. "You have to leave," came Jay's voice, and I looked to see which of us he was talking to. Her.

"Go. Please go. I'll call you." She stiffened and started to say something, but he cut her off. "Please," he said, and she turned and left.

The front door slammed behind her, and Jay walked out of the kitchen. I sat alone at the table, trying to figure things out. He was still seeing her? He was going to call her? When had he told her we didn't have this kind of relationship? Before we actually did, or after?

One thing, at least, was clear. She was gone, and I was here. But there was still plenty that Jay would have to explain over the rest of the weekend. I waited a bit for him to come back to the kitchen, then went and found him pacing back and forth in the bedroom.

"She told me she threw out the key," he said, extremely agitated, still pacing.

"But . . ."

"I can't," he said. "Not now. Please, go home."

Suddenly that felt like the right idea.

"You may want to change your locks," was all I said as I got dressed.

I drove home with fierce concentration on the road, trying to keep my thoughts under control. Had he really broken up with her months earlier? Had he really thought she'd thrown out the key? Would he call me? Would he call her? Was he right now telling her I'd just left? Did the answers to any of these questions still matter?

He called me the next morning.

"I talked to her," he said. "That won't happen again. And the locks are changed."

Five happy months later, it was fall—time for holiday plans to be nailed down, and time for me to take my head out of the sand.

Nearly a year had passed since I'd told Jay, "I don't go out with men who have girlfriends." He and I went out regularly, rarely missed a goodnight phone call, bought each other thinking-of-you gifts, held hands across restaurant tables. But though he'd met some of my friends, I'd met none of his. We almost never went out on Saturdays. For all I could tell, I was still his little secret on the side.

He was driving me home one evening, when, fervidly hoping this would turn out okay, I asked, "What are you doing for Thanksgiving?"

"Nothing elaborate," he said. "Getting together with friends."

With friends. His old code for "with Eve."

Perhaps I asked, "With the Kramers?" I might even have said, "With Eve?" but I think not, because all he said was, "How about you?"

"I'm having it at my place," I said. "The girls, Michael and Marina, some other friends."

"Sounds nice," he said. He drove with his left hand, his right covering mine on the seat between us.

"I'd love you to join us," I said. "Your kids too, if they're coming up."

"That would be nice," he answered, "but I'm all set."

When we pulled up at my house, I said something utterly unoriginal but exactly right.

"This isn't working for me anymore."

I felt preternaturally calm.

"I want three things, Jay. I want us to have Thanksgiving together. I want to meet the Kramers. And I want to be your Saturday night girl."

A long time passed before he said in a voice devoid of life, "I can't." He shut off the engine and turned toward me, expecting a conversation, but I got out of the car.

As I moved to close the door, I told him, "I hope you'll find you can after all, but if not, please don't call."

There was an unsplintered world in which colleagues said good morning in the same old way and daughters asked for car keys as they always had, but that world was beyond my reach. Alone in my own world, I prowled the house by night and feigned busyness at work by day, all the while feeling I was elsewhere but not knowing where.

Days, then a few weeks, and then a couple of months passed. Slowly, one tentative filament at a time, I'd begun to reconnect to the world of others when a letter arrived, addressed in Jay's familiar spikey hand. It was many pages long, with propulsive writing running edge to edge. He'd ended things with Eve, it said. It had been harder than he'd expected, but he'd seen it through, and they were decisively over. He'd also realized, he hoped not too late, how much I meant to him. He asked if we could meet.

There was love in those pages, and hope, and apprehension about where I stood. I had my own apprehensions, about where I stood and about my ability to absorb another breakup. For several weeks, I didn't answer. Ultimately, I decided there was enough in his letter that sounded new, and I agreed to meet.

Were we old friends? People who used to know each other? A couple in love? When he opened his door, neither of us knew.

He moved aside to let me in but stood stiffly, no hand on my waist to bring me close. I stepped through carefully, not grazing any part of him. Shaka bounded over, berserk with surprise and joy, his whole golden body wagging.

"Good boy," I said, scratching him under his collar the way he liked. I was grateful for the chance to compose myself. "Good boy. I missed you too."

"He and I both missed you," said Jay, and finally we were looking at each other. Skirting anything that mattered, we talked about where to talk. We settled on the living room and headed for separate chairs, each of us markedly avoiding the couch and its memories of closeness. Then we talked for a very long time.

Months earlier, I'd told him I needed to have Thanksgiving together, to meet the Kramers, and to be his declared girlfriend. Thanksgiving had come and gone and would have to wait, but the following Saturday we went out with the Kramers, and from then on, unambiguously a couple, we met each other's friends and colleagues. Jay asked me to go with him to England to meet his parents in January, six weeks away, and from there to visit his daughter, who was spending a year in Israel. I said yes.

Poor Jeanie. She'd given her heart to Brown University, and Brown had broken it by rejecting her for early admission and deferring a decision until April. Adding insult to misery, she now had to spend her winter break applying to other schools. She asked Jay to help her with her essays, and for several nights he came for dinner, after which they got to work. Sitting with the newspaper and a cup of tea, I'd hear their voices and the clacking of my Selectric and feel deeply peaceful. My boyfriend was a man I could bring into my daughters' lives with total confidence.

Jay and I left for England just a few days after Jeanie mailed off her applications. His parents, South African expats who'd moved to London many decades earlier, were in their nineties, but I'd been off the mark with my expectation of a frail couple keeping each other company over tea and telly. The two of them seemed to inhabit their apartment with hardly a connection to each other. Except for meals, they tended to occupy themselves in separate rooms.

His mother, a tiny drill bit of a woman, sat in an upholstered chair, her eyes on the television. No kiss, no warm hug, not even getting up to greet her son, freshly arrived from America. "Would you get me my sweater from the bedroom, Jay," was all she said, talking to him as though he were a child. She turned her attention back to the BBC without acknowledging my presence. I sat down and watched TV with her for a while, until, trying to engage, I asked if I might help with dinner.

"Why don't you set the table," she said. When I was done, she surveyed my work. "I just love the way Americans set a table," she cooed. "But we do it *this* way!" And she snatched a teaspoon and dessert fork from the sides of a plate and slammed them down above it.

Jay's father was a shrunken rendition of the grim-faced, iron-spined man I'd seen in photos. At dinner he talked to Jay about current events. His mother talked about goings-on in the far-flung extended family. Neither seemed particularly interested in what Jay was up to or curious about this woman he now had in his life.

When the two of us were alone, I bristled at how cold they were toward him. "They're old, doll," he said, which to me was no explanation at all.

Warmth and interest aplenty came the night before we left London for Israel, though. A swarm of his English cousins descended on his parents' apartment, overjoyed to see Jay and eager to meet me. Only a few moments after she arrived, his cousin Marilyn whispered in my ear, "I don't know anything about you yet, but I already love you for making Jay so happy."

In Israel, Jay's daughter would no doubt have preferred having him to herself, but she seemed resigned to my presence and was clearly trying to be gracious. Unlike her brothers, she'd met me a few times before, when she was back in Boston on college breaks. I'd even taken her out in my car a few times to practice for the road test for her driver's license. In those days, though, I'd been a family friend. Now I was her father's girlfriend.

"How was London?" she asked Jay. "Did you have a good visit with Granny and Grandpa?"

"They threw a nice party with the cousins, but beyond that . . ." and he trailed off with a little shrug. "They're old," she quickly interjected. Silent in the back seat of our rental car, I thought to myself, They're old? That again?

After our visit with his daughter, Jay and I had dinner plans with Shayna and Izik, friends I'd met through my grandmother Minnie. I'd known Shayna since I was a young teen, before she'd married Izik and her family had moved from the US to Israel, and I was excited about reconnecting with them and introducing them to Jay.

They lived in Bnei Brak, a town near Tel Aviv that was populated almost entirely by haredim, very observant orthodox Jews. The town itself reflected their strict religious practices, with businesses closed and driving prohibited on the Sabbath, as well as accommodations facilitating the separation of men and women where their custom required.

Walking from the bus stop, we took a left and expected to be on a quiet residential street softly settling into dinnertime. Instead, we found ourselves on the edge of a crowd. It seemed to be keeping watch on the house we'd thought was Izik and Shayna's. There must have been thirty people—men with sidelocks, big black hats, and long black coats; women with wigs and headscarves, dressed in modest long-sleeved clothing. I'd known in general about the haredim, but only now did I start to understand how profoundly their unequivocal adherence to religious law shaped their lives. Having been just moments earlier a cheerful woman happily anticipating dinner with her boyfriend and old friends, I suddenly realized how much of an outsider I was in this unfamiliar territory.

We were wondering what to do next, when a man in the crowd noticed us and I heard him say to another, "*Iz zee Minnie's eynikl?*" I don't know much Yiddish, but it didn't take much to understand what he was saying. "Is she Minnie's granddaughter?"

As the question rippled through the crowd, they all turned and looked at us. There I was, a woman with neither wig nor headscarf, in clothing I'd thought was modest but now understood wasn't nearly modest enough, arriving with her boyfriend in a community where even engaged couples meet only when chaperoned and are forbidden to touch each other.

More than that, I was facing a crowd who somehow knew about Minnie and seemed to be waiting for me.

What were we into here?

At that moment, the door to the house opened. What a relief it was to see Izik standing on the stoop at the top of the steps. He said something to the crowd in Yiddish, and they parted like the Red Sea, creating a one-person-wide path to the stairs leading up to the open door. Then he called to Jay and me, in English, "Welcome! Come! Come!" As we walked forward, with me in the lead, some of the women reached out and touched me gently. All around us we heard, "Minnie's eynikl. Minnie's eynikl."

Shayna appeared in the doorway and reached out her hand to me. "Marsha! Welcome," she said. "And is this your husband?"

"Yes!" I answered, without so much as turning around to shoot Jay a question with my eyes, but he was right with me. 'Hi, Shayna. Hi, Izik," he said. "I'm Jay. It's great to meet you."

In Yiddish, Izik formally introduced us to the assembly, and several people called out blessings. Then Shayna and he said goodnight to them all and ushered us into their home, closing the door behind us.

They were the most gracious of hosts, and their children and grandchildren—very many of each—were cheerful and utterly engaging. We couldn't keep track of which kids belonged to which parents, especially since Shayna and some of her daughters had had children at about the same time.

When most of the children had been taken home to bed and just a few adults sat around the table, I could finally ask about that crowd.

"How did you meet Shayna's family," I'd once asked Minnie, and she told me that she'd met Shayna's mother when their family arrived in America and had helped them settle in. I learned from Shayna that there was much more to the story.

When Jews escaping Europe during WWII were finally allowed into the US, Minnie collected household furnishings and clothing for the arriving immigrants and went down to the docks to meet their ships. If they arrived before their housing was arranged, she took them into her own home, where she and Max treated them like family. Among the people waiting outside Shayna's house had been several Minnie had escorted into their new life in America. Many of their offspring were there too; to them, Minnie was a hero they'd heard about since childhood. They'd all gathered to honor a direct descendent of the woman they credited with saving their lives and the lives of their generations to come.

Minnie died at 103, only a year after Jay and I went to Israel. I was told that throughout Bnei Brak, many sat shiva for her.

While we were in Israel, a number of Jay's South African cousins happened to be there for the bar mitzvah of one of his Israeli cousins' kids, and we met up with them at the home of one of the local families. The place was packed. How many cousins does this man have? I wondered.

It was a great evening. Everyone was in high spirits, and I readily felt like part of the gang. Most of the South Africans hadn't seen Jay in decades, and they held him close and clapped him on the back. "Howzit, Jay?" "You're looking bloody good, Jay."

That evening, I discovered that Jay's accent wasn't the South African accent he'd grown up speaking but was rather the accent of his youth smoothed into something softer by his many years in England and America. In the presence of his South African cousins, it reverted to the original. His voice and even his laugh became deep and throaty and lost some of its warmth. At times I could hardly understand what he was saying. "This is eerie," I said, joking around. "It's like someone else has taken over his body."

– 19 –

MOVING ON

MAYBE IT'S A GENETIC THING, OR a gender thing. I'm one of those people who often feel cold when others feel fine, and once I get chilled, it's a real struggle to warm up. After the warmth of Israel, the Boston winter hit me harder than ever. We were on our way to a restaurant, walking fast in the frigid air—Jay hatless, gloveless, comfortable; I with down coat, wool hat, glove liners under my gloves, shivering. Suddenly he took my elbow and turned me into a furrier shop we were passing.

"Let's get you a real hat," he said, and he asked the proprietor to show me some particularly warm ones. I was dazzled by the store and out of my league. "Let me get this for you," Jay said. "Please, doll. I really want to. Look at you. You're suffering."

The hat was majestic, a spectacle really, with a penumbra of long silvery fur all around and a lushness I could bury my fingers in. In truth, it was too flamboyant for me, but I wore it often, big as it was, because he loved to see me warm and I loved to see him love it.

About two months later, Jay asked, "Do you think we should get married?"

"I do," I said. "Do you?"

"I do," he said. "I was thinking maybe October."

"October's perfect," I said.

No grand flourish or bended knee. Just a fifteen-second conversation, and it was all we needed. We'd understood for some time that we'd be spending the rest of our lives together. We'd been missing only a plan to formalize it.

It had been five years since Lydia's death, and we knew Jay's kids would have complicated reactions to his getting remarried. We assumed both my girls would be excited, but just in case, we decided we'd each tell our own kids individually. I went to see Ellen at college and gave her our big news over lunch.

"About time!" she said.

I told Jeanie after dinner that same night. She yelled "Hurray!!" and threw herself on me in a bear hug.

"Wait," she said, pulling back. "Why isn't Jay here for this?" and she ran to the phone to ask him to come over.

Jay's kids reacted worse than we'd expected. They turned down his invitations to Boston and resisted when he said he wanted to visit them. One of his sons, fishing for information and also making clear where he stood, said, "Why are you so set on a visit? It's not like you're getting married or anything."

In the end, Jay told each of them by phone. His sons lobbied hard for him to break off the engagement, and when that didn't work, one of them tried to convince me I should run while I had the chance. "He's a spendthrift," this son said. "He goes off on wild sprees. You could lose all your money." He reeled off a string of equally unfounded shortcomings of

Jay's while I stood there, undeterred but struck by the depth of his passion and impressed with his ingenuity.

"It's sad that Jay's kids are digging in like this," Betty Kramer told me, "but not surprising. Hopefully they'll come around."

I wasn't so sure they would. "I think it's harder for them than I expected, seeing Jay with another woman," I said.

At Fidelity something was afoot. Only two weeks into Jay's and my engagement, Nita, my boss, said she might need to reach me over the weekend. As it happened, it was a weekend I'd be at Jay's. I gave her his number, and we stayed in so I wouldn't miss her call.

It came on Sunday. The next morning, she told me, she'd be announcing a reorganization at work. I was getting a big promotion, my areas of responsibility tripling. Not long afterward, there was big news of a different sort. Our Boston, Dallas, Salt Lake City, and New York operations would be consolidated into a single location in Covington, Kentucky, right across the river from Cincinnati. All my departments would be moving, and I'd be on the small team responsible for making the consolidation go smoothly.

"I'll stay as long as you want," I told Nita, "but I personally can't relocate."

Moving the operations required our planning team to attend to literally thousands of details. Hundreds of employees and workflows were affected. For the employees, Fidelity mobilized a platoon of real estate agents and job recruiters to help find homes for those relocating and jobs for their partners.

Nearly all staff who couldn't relocate were offered new Fidelity jobs in the Boston area.

As for the workflows, for each type of transaction that shareholders might want to do, such as buying or selling shares, there would come a specific hour when all processing stopped in Boston, Dallas, Salt Lake City, and New York and simultaneously started up in Kentucky. Federal regulations required most transactions to be processed on the day instructions arrived, and we knew that despite enormous outreach to shareholders about the change, hundreds of letters of instruction would arrive in the present locations, where processing capabilities would have been shut off.

Failure to manage the switchovers properly could in one day fling Fidelity into regulatory noncompliance hugely larger than Shawmut's had been. The stakes were high not only for the company but also, we knew, for our little transition management group. After obsessive planning and test runs, we were thrilled and relieved when one stage after another went smoothly.

The consolidation was almost finished when trouble came in the form of more reorganization. Nita was made president of a different subsidiary, and a brassy guy named Joe arrived from the Salt Lake City office to be our new boss. He was the kind of guy who joked about his sexual exploits in staff meetings, where I was the only woman. In no time, he fired one of my colleagues and me to bring in his own people. Like him, they wanted to leave the now diminished Salt Lake City location and come to Boston, the seat of power.

Fifteen years earlier, when I'd just left Peter and was supporting my family paycheck by paycheck, this would have been catastrophic. Now I had savings, a strong resume, and a network of people who would support my job search. In fact, I'd started looking for a new position as soon as I'd ruled out moving to Kentucky. The head of marketing at Fidelity had been talking to me about a new job, but with each conversation I'd become less enthusiastic. Outside of work, I served on the boards of some not-for-profits and found it more satisfying than the corporate work I'd done since business school.

It was three weeks before our wedding. Jay's kids were working and self-sufficient. Jeanie was starting college, and Ellen had two years to go. Jay and I did some figuring and decided we could afford my doing what I really wanted to do, which was to leave the corporate world and work in the not-for-profit sector.

– 20 –

DANCING IN THE KITCHEN

WHEN WE MARRIED, WE'D KNOWN each other thirteen years. For three of those, we were colleagues; for five, former colleagues who lunched. We were mostly out of touch the year after Lydia's death, and after one more year of spotty contact, we reconnected by sheer luck when Jay was let go from Teradyne. Then we spent three years bumpily falling in love.

They weren't easy, those three years. I was in my forties and Jay in his fifties. We had habits. We had histories. We had kids. When we got engaged, mine were eighteen and twenty, not yet fledged. His were twenty-three, twenty-seven, and thirty-one, loyal to their mother and resolutely against our plans.

Love had come neither quickly nor smoothly, but once we had it, there was glory in it, and that was the abundant generosity of spirit between us. When we differed on hard things, like kids, like money, we were hospitable to the other's views, trusted they were proffered in good faith, and worked sincerely to understand them. We exalted each other's virtuosities and gave each other our total attention, one of the deepest kinds of caring there is.

From our early courtship, when I learned his ex-girlfriend was not precisely ex, to our wedding three years later, when his kids sulked and gave mine the cold shoulder, we resolved wrenching contentions and grew wiser from each other, closer, more flexible, serene and brave with the knowledge that we each had someone who would always show up for us. Feeling deeply understood and unfailingly supported, we lived simultaneously in our own little bubble and in a world enlarged for each of us by the other.

Despite all this, there was one intractable contention, and that was a prenup. Jay insisted we have one to assure that his kids would get their proper inheritance from Lydia. I agreed with the concept but not with the way he wanted to calculate it. Under his method, much less of his ongoing earnings than mine would count as marital earnings, though our salaries were the same.

"My kids will go to war if we don't do this," he said.

"Let them," I said. "They'll see. It will all be okay. You know I won't cheat your kids, any more than you'd cheat mine."

He couldn't drop it. I couldn't live with it. There was no middle ground. Finally, I signed it with unhidden resentment and a few days to myself. Over time I discovered that I could live with it after all, in the way one lives with smog, usually forgetting about it but sometimes aware of the danger.

For the first six months we lived in a construction site as the work we were doing to convert Jay's house into our house fell behind schedule. The worst of it was getting through the Boston winter with just a blue tarp where an outside wall should have been. Spring finally rewarded us with warmth, a house we loved, and the expectation that we could withstand anything.

I became the chief operating officer of a nonprofit that ran a couple hundred programs for adults with severe mental illness or developmental disabilities. At the same time, the startup Jay had joined after leaving Teradyne was growing fast. Both of us had demanding jobs, and we both loved working. We talked about work problems with each other all the time, enjoying the conceit that each of our companies was getting two for the price of one.

Our private jokes; the way we conveyed messages to each other with the twitch of an eyebrow; our personal vocabulary, in which the word *rubbish* unexpectedly became a term of endearment. We loved love as lovers do, as though we'd invented it.

"When you were a schoolgirl in Indiana," he'd say, "and I was in the South African army, who'd have thought we'd ever find each other?"

"We were always going to find each other," I'd say. "You're the love of my life."

We danced in the kitchen, and not just in the first years, when we were daffy with romance. Jay would tap my shoulder, or I'd tap his arm, and we'd put down the sponge and the towel and dance cheek to cheek, with me humming the music in his ear. Then we'd turn back to our cleaning up, love-hearted.

"You pulled me through," he'd say. "I was stuck somewhere awful, and you got me out."

"You pulled yourself out," I'd say. "All I did was wait for you."

"Do you know what Jay told me about your girls?" his sister-in-law asked me.

"What?" I said, though I knew full well. He told everyone.

"He said that when he married you, Ellen and Jeanie were a special bonus he'd never imagined. I swear he had tears in his eyes."

My girls and Jay had welcomed each other from the start, and they grew ever closer over the years. Jeanie introduced us to her friends as "my parents." When Ellen got married, she wanted Jay to join me in walking her down the aisle, and she created a lovely, different role for Peter. But Jay's kids stayed detached. In the construction on our house, we'd added bedrooms in anticipation of visits from several of our kids at once, but his brood rarely came, and they never stayed over.

"They're a tough bunch." Dave Kramer told me. "It's not about you." He was standing in our kitchen, carving the turkey he'd made in his beloved smoker. It was yet another Thanksgiving with our friends and my girls, but with none of Jay's kids.

"I can't imagine what it's like to have lost their mother as they did," I said, "but I confess I'd hoped that by now they'd be a little warmer."

– 21 –
APPARITION

TEN YEARS PASSED. HOUSES, TRIPS, jobs, come and gone. Children married, grandchildren born. But still, when he glanced up from the paper, when the lights came on after a movie, when I came through the door, he looked at me and his face showed love, and, like a mirror, mine showed the same to him. Ten years already, and, as each year before had, this one felt like our best yet.

Everyone was doing well. Ellen was working in Chicago, and Jeanie was in grad school. Jay's kids now had kids of their own. I'd left the mental health organization and become chief operating officer at the New England Organ Bank, where I devised a new program that significantly increased organ donations. Forever the most rewarding experience in my career, this initiative ultimately saved hundreds of lives and became a model for a national program.

After the organ bank, I went out on my own and started a consulting practice. Jay's company had been sold, and he'd agreed to stay on for a year to help with the transition to new management. Now that year was up, and he was starting his own consulting practice. Our plan was to eventually shrink our practices and gradually slide into retirement.

We'd just moved from the house to a condo and were finding it magical that snow was plowed and garbage carried out without our ever thinking about it. We still loved work and work-talk, and now we had the flexibility to also enjoy small pleasures like daytime movies or going out for breakfast. We were fully content.

Over the years, I'd tried to envision his boyhood in South Africa, but my sense of it was patchy. Jay had tried several times to describe the stunning scenery, the deep night skies, the magnificence of the bush and the animals that lived there. Of his own daily life, however, he spoke little. I did know that as a youngster he'd seen servants beaten and had witnessed a white man set a man-killing dog on a Black man, but he'd never give me more details.

Like so many whites, his family were beneficiaries, though not advocates, of apartheid, which started when he was five and lasted all the way through his army service, college, and another thirty years after he'd left South Africa for good. They were Jews in a place where antisemitism coexisted naturally with racism. Jay's limp came from no accident. A hate-spewing student had grabbed his leg during wrestling practice and intentionally twisted the knee until it was seriously damaged. Perhaps the coach hadn't noticed, or perhaps he was indifferent. No matter. The results were the same. Jewboy, varsity in six sports, was out of commission.

Photos showed that even as a young man, Jay had a sensitive face, the face of someone who might write sonnets.

Who could imagine such a face in such a place? It astonished me that he said it was in the South African army, of all places, that he first found peace. At night he'd lie on the ground, looking at the stars, listening to the noises of his beloved bushveldt, and loving the army for the camaraderie and the reliable orderliness.

Jay's father died, and his mother, well into her nineties and infirm, left England and went back to South Africa to live in a nursing home near her daughter's house in a Johannesburg suburb. Jay had largely avoided his homeland for close to forty years, but, increasingly, he wanted to see it again and show it to me. With his mother back there and likely near the end of her life, he decided the time was right for us to make the trip.

The rental car clerk at the Johannesburg airport gave us a sheet of instructions and a warning to take them seriously. We were to keep all valuables, even sunglasses, out of sight to deter someone from smashing the windshield at a stop sign to steal them. We were to hide all maps, a signal we weren't from there and could easily be victimized. We weren't to take side streets, ask directions, stop unless absolutely necessary, or drive at night. Had I been traveling without Jay, I would have turned around and gone home the instant I saw that list.

Apartheid had left in its wake monumental extremes of wealth and poverty and a terrifying crime rate. Multitudes lived in squalid settlements or on the streets, while homes of many of the well-to-do stood behind high walls topped with coils of barbed wire. Heavy iron gates were opened from inside these fortresses, after a careful look at a security screen. People had been trapped in those posh streets and robbed and beaten. It had happened to Lydia's father, in his nineties.

The visits with Jay's family were distressing. His mother seemed indifferent to our arrival and talked only about how the South African relatives were treating her like royalty since her return from the diaspora. His brother-in-law went on self-righteously about how troublesome and ungrateful "the Blacks" were. In their opulent home tended by servants, his sister railed about how hard it was to find proper servants, well within earshot of those allegedly un-proper.

I'd been looking forward to meeting Jay's South African family, and I was shocked that this was who they were. Jay wasn't surprised by their talk, but he'd thought he was prepared for it. It hit him as hard as it hit me, and, with tense jaws and an impulse to run, we said our goodbyes and began our real vacation.

First came two different safaris in two different terrains: out in the jeeps before sunrise to see the animals before they disappeared, as we ourselves did, to nap through the hottest part of the day; then back in the jeeps to see the twilight animals and nocturnals emerge. After dinner back at our accomodations, we fell asleep to the roars of distant lions, waking pre-dawn to get back into the jeeps and steep ourselves again in the wonder of the bushveldt.

Next we traveled from Johannesburg to Cape Town, driving through overpoweringly gorgeous scenery: mighty cliffs and rock formations, beaches that sparkled in the light, transparent turquoise water edged with pure white foam. We drank delicious wines, ate succulent food, and took in shops and street markets. I couldn't get enough of the music.

Street groups were everywhere, singing with six, seven, eight harmonies in irresistible rhythms. Pulling along a more-than-willing Jay, I followed the singers from corner to corner and happily gave them money.

"Finally," Jay said. "I've finally been able to show you where I come from," and I thought I had at least a small sense of how wrenching it must have been for him to give up the parts of South Africa he loved in order to escape the rest.

Back in Boston, in the charmed aftermath of that trip, Jay opened the door one evening at the sound of my keys, said, "Hi, doll," as always, and took my bag. "Whew," I said, unzipping my boots. "Long day."

Suddenly his face whitened, tightened. His lips sneered, nostrils flared, eyes narrowed with menace. I felt him as an advancing warrior, though his feet never moved. Then, so quickly that I doubted I'd seen what I'd seen, Jay was again just Jay.

"Want to eat in or out?" he asked.

I banished the warrior from my mind, uneasily at first and then with no effort at all, as he fell into the past. It would be some time before he appeared again, and by then so much would have changed that a sudden distortion of Jay's face would be just one of many things I couldn't absorb.

The first to go were the little gestures, the pat on my shoulder when he walked by, the wink when our eyes met across a room. He became snappish, then surly. He stopped wanting to talk and avoided friends. When the Catholic Church sexual abuse scandal dominated the *Boston Globe*, this empathetic man disdained the victims, insisting there was no such thing as suppressed memories. I started coming home gingerly, not knowing which Jay would be there, mine or the churlish one.

After a few months, he accepted a consulting gig in Baltimore without talking to me about it first. "What are you fussing about?" he said. "I'll fly out Monday mornings and come back Tuesday nights. What's the big deal?"

It *was* a big deal, this abandonment of our way of deciding things, and it was also true that I'd become a fusser. Suddenly, in the eleventh year of our marriage, we were far from our best selves.

There came a Sunday when I found him packing for Baltimore in the afternoon instead of the evening. "I'm flying out tonight instead of tomorrow morning," he said. "This way I can get a full night's sleep before I go to the office."

Okay, I thought, that's reasonable. Before long, though, he was leaving Sunday and coming back not on Tuesday but on Wednesday, then Thursday, then Friday.

"Hey, honey, what's going on?" I asked. "What *is* all this?"

He shrugged. "All what?"

My question became a scold. "What IS all this! Don't you see you're shutting me out?" On one low night, we had an hour-long wrangle of a type we'd never had before, I with fifty ways to say, "What IS all this," and he with fifty ways to say, "All WHAT?" Things got briefly better after that. I think we scared ourselves.

One Saturday, I walked into the bedroom, said something ordinary, and, for the second time, out came the twisted-faced warrior, chest puffed, arms akimbo. His eyes were slits. His lips moved, but silently. His feet were firmly planted, but I felt him coming at me. I might have cried out, "Stop!"

Again, the specter vanished quickly. Jay's body relaxed, and his blue eyes looked at me in such a normal way that I relaxed too.

"What were you doing with your face?" I asked.

"What do you mean?" He touched his cheek. "Is something wrong with my face?"

I told myself that he was worn out from the going and coming, the packing and unpacking; that things would get better when the Baltimore engagement was over and he was back in Boston. But when the Baltimore work finished, nothing improved. We seesawed between the good old days and the bad new ones. Hope. Letdown. Hope. Letdown. The cycle wore me down and wakened a reflex that had been dormant for decades: the defeating watchfulness for the bad thing that might burst forth at any moment.

But then our little world got better. Jay teamed up with Hojun, an MIT engineer who'd designed a new type of medical device, and they decided to start a new company to manufacture and sell it. Much of their planning happened at our kitchen table, and gradually they pulled me in. The first thing I did for them was find suitable space for the new enterprise and negotiate the lease. Soon I started going to their office a couple of afternoons a week to help with strategic planning and hiring. As each of my consulting engagements wrapped up, I took on more work with Jay and Hojun. Ultimately, we formalized my role as the third member of the management team.

It was a heady time. Every decision was consequential, from where to manufacture to whether it was better to hire a sales force or to contract with a distributor. The staff was small, close-knit, and energized with possibility. At home, Jay and I were in love again.

Then Warrior returned. Every few weeks or so he would swell and snarl and quickly disappear on no cue that I could see. I said I felt bullied. Jay said I was making things up. We started couples' therapy, and before long we had three therapists—his, mine, and ours.

"Honestly, I don't know what to make of you two," said Bea. She was our couples' therapist. The obvious bond she saw between Jay and me didn't jibe with the different stories we told. I'd describe an argument we'd had when Jay was in warrior mode, and he'd say, "Maybe I was annoyed, but nothing like that."

"Look, you two clearly care for each other," Bea said, "but you've stopped listening to each other," and she started assigning us homework. Once she told us to have a weekly date night and dress up for each other. Another time she told us to end each day by saying three things we loved about the other. It sounded like something from a supermarket magazine. "Experts Reveal Their Secrets: Restore Your Love Life In Just Two Weeks!" It drove me crazy.

I told myself I'd give Bea one more month, but at our appointment just a week later, everything changed.

On the first floor of her Victorian home, Bea's office, in a room originally built to be a parlor, was what a nineteenth century architecture buff might call an important room—dark woodwork, small sculptures that spoke of exotic travel, an expansive oriental carpet more refined than diminished by its signs of wear. If there was a white noise machine, I don't recall it. Certainly the room's upholstered stateliness and substantial wooden doors gave the impression that the most sensitive of topics could safely be ventured there.

As always, I arrived first and sat on the couch under the windows. Jay took his customary chair across from me. Bea sat to the side, where she could observe us both. She asked how our week had gone, and, as always, we gave very different accounts. Yet again, the session felt pointless. I checked my watch and idly traced the carvings on her chair with my eyes.

Suddenly Jay was snarling at me, spewing words in the same guttural voice he'd slid into with his South African cousins. He glowered and grimaced, leaned forward and gripped the arms of his chair, looking ready to catapult himself at me. I pressed myself deep into the back of the couch and kept my eyes on his, afraid that if I looked away, he'd spring. Then all at once it was over. He sat back in his chair and looked normal.

Bea was transformed and in command, her face grave. She had me describe what I'd just seen. My voice shook. She asked Jay if he agreed with my description. Not at all.

"What were you saying just now, before we paused?" she asked, and he didn't know.

Something big had shifted. I'd wished for this, for Bea to witness what I'd been seeing at home, but now I felt a cold foreboding. Jay looked too naive, too unaware that this was serious. Instinctively, I crossed the room and took his hand.

"We can't leave it here," Bea said, "but our time's up, and my next client is waiting. Can you come back in an hour?" We went to a coffee shop and sat silently, holding each other's hands across the table and never touching our coffee.

By the time we returned to Bea's, she'd already alerted Jay's therapist. She got him back on the phone and put him on speaker. It was late on a Friday afternoon, and he and Jay scheduled an appointment for early Monday morning.

Both therapists felt there was some risk that the shock of learning he'd had violent episodes could cause Jay to panic or become despondent over the weekend. They briefly discussed hospitalizing him but concluded there were too many drawbacks. His therapist proposed that Jay and I spend the weekend in a hotel, where we could have a quiet couple of days and stick close to each other, with our needs taken care of by others.

Bea said Jay might become agitated or excessively withdrawn and asked if I'd be able to raise an alarm should either appear serious, especially if it looked like he might hurt himself. Pressed together on her couch, Jay and I had become like a single piece of wood, just another sculpture in the room, insensate as other people's conversations hovered nearby. I cleared my throat and said yes. Numbly following orders we didn't understand, we called a local hotel and made a reservation.

New terms, *dissociative disorder* and *PTSD*, entered our vocabulary, and soon we had a mantra too. "All I want," Jay said, "is to get to the other side of this together." Over and over we told each other we would do exactly that. Air, water, shelter, food, and The Other Side Together—we needed them equally.

My own therapist felt unequipped to help me through the complexity of our situation, and we stopped meeting. Jay saw his therapist more often than before and started medications.

Our sessions with Bea continued, but now there was no discord between Jay and me. We went for support and advice on the challenge we faced together. We still had no explanation for Warrior's appearances.

I felt protective of Jay, always on duty. Long after our weekend at the hotel, my radar stayed locked on him. If he seemed flustered or abrupt, was he "extremely agitated"? If he spent a whole evening at his computer, was he "excessively withdrawn"? The therapists' warning, "He might hurt himself," weighed on me, and I lived with an ambient fear that at any moment he actually would.

Months went by. One Friday I arrived at Bea's for our regular appointment and found Jay's car already there. Strangely, the door to her office was wide open. Jay was sitting, almost lying, in my usual spot on the couch. He looked like he'd come down with an awful flu.

"Come in," said Bea. "Jay has something to say."

I went in warily, slow with dread, never taking my eyes from his face.

"Jay? Honey? What is it?" I asked. "What's wrong?"

It was Bea who answered. "Jay's done some important work with his therapist," she said, "and he's got something to tell you."

And my dear love, his face wearing the grief of a child undone, said he'd come to remember horrible things done to him from when he was five or even younger and into his teens, by his own parents, sometimes in front of others, all of whom kept silent.

Before he could finish what he'd meant to say, he caved in on himself and shook with sobs, hiding his face in his hands.

In less than a breath I was with him on the couch. I pulled him upright, forced his hands away and held his face in my own two hands. Then I wrapped my arms around his shuddering body as he turned into my shoulder and wept.

– 22 –

A TRIGGER PULLED

Four years earlier, unnoticed in the moment, a shock of news—his father's death—had cracked a vault buried deep within Jay, and the memories interred there had slowly seeped out. Once released, they'd breached the barricades protecting him from his own early life and desecrated his view of who he was. No wonder he'd so adamantly dismissed the church victims' recovered memories, with the scent of his own growing stronger.

Jay's parents doing unconscionable things to him as a toddler, a youngster, a teen. Once I heard his memories, they were my memories too. Mostly they came for us in the night, not like some hazy recollection but with the force of real life. He'd thrash in his sleep or cry out and wake shaking, and I'd wrap around him and whisper, "Shhh. It's okay. You're okay."

"I know. I know, doll," he'd murmur, his eyes still closed.

Long after he was sleeping again, I'd lie there haunted by images of scenes that should have gotten his parents horsewhipped. That they'd lived long, smug lives, unexposed and unpunished, consumed me. They'd been proud, no doubt, of the inheritance they'd leave, but their true legacy was those secrets, flowing toxic and icy through the veins of their beautiful boy. As the writhing of sleepless nights allows one to do, again and again I brought the two of them back to life and took barbarous revenge.

Now we understood that everyday things could trigger a flashback and summon Warrior, that Jay could lose the here and now, lose sight of me, and be back in terrible times. To heal, he'd have to relive his abusive childhood and somehow maintain the faith that one day he'd live in peace with his real past. In the meantime, I would need enough faith for both of us. And I had that faith. Even while absorbing his terrors and feeling my fury, I saw his recovery of the memories as a breakthrough. At least now we knew what we had to get to the other side of.

If ours had been a normal problem—say, a blonde in Baltimore—how straightforward things would have been. I'd have told my friends, and they'd have known exactly how to rally around me. But our problem wasn't normal. To outsiders, even to people devoted to us, Jay's tragedy would conjure up lurid images that would adhere to him forever. He'd be not just Jay, but Jay, the guy whose parents. . . .

Can you imagine being carried back as an adult to a forgotten childhood like his? I couldn't then, and I can't now. I felt responsible for protecting his privacy until he could face his own history and decide for himself whether and how to share it. Under orders from myself to act with friends and family as though things were normal, I found I had no stamina to pretend. I pulled back from everyone except Jay, shrinking my world into a narrow tunnel with our home at one end and our little company at the other.

Without intending to or even noticing, I was the one who became excessively withdrawn.

After a few months of this, my daughter Ellen flew in with something on her mind. "You hardly call or email," she said. "It's like you don't want to talk to me."

"Jay's having a hard time with something painful and private in his family," I said, "but it's not my story to tell. I didn't realize I was so absorbed in it."

"Well, whatever it is," she said, "it looks like now it's your story too."

Of course, she was right. I told her what was happening, and that evening I called Jeanie and also Worth, who started to cry.

"I'm sorry," she wept. "It's just that you were both so happy."

Something unthinkable. Jay started criticizing me in public, and if I shot him a signal to pull back, he called me out for everyone to hear. "Why are you poking me? You don't like what I'm saying?" Of course I'd heard him angry before, or frustrated, but never loud. "I understand, doll," he might say, "but I still think . . ." or "Hey doll, I hate to say this but . . ." Even when he threw up his hands and said, "For crying out loud, doll," he said it with energy but not volume.

In our worst argument, about the prenup, we hadn't yelled. Now Jay was a shouter. At a fundraiser for a nonprofit on whose board I served, he made a scene over, of all things, whether we should check our coats. People stopped their conversations and looked up. My cheeks burning, I turned my back to them and faced the coat-check window as he marched off into the crowd.

He was testy with his kids too, and he started avoiding them. The change was dramatic. He'd regularly talked to them for an hour or more, and now he would let the phone ring or make excuses and hang up quickly.

"He's avoiding his kids," I told Bea on the phone. "And with me, he keeps ratcheting things up. When I don't rise to the bait, he comes back at me harder." She listened somberly and took a moment before answering.

"I think Jay loves you very much," she said, then, more slowly, "but that doesn't always matter."

There is danger here. I'm practically sniffing the air.

"It does in our case," I said crisply. "You've heard him. All he wants is for us to get to the other side of this together."

"Yes," she answered. "I know. And I believe he means it. But staying in the marriage might be too hard for him."

Into my hard-edged silence she added, "And he might not be able to pull the trigger. This ratcheting up he's doing—whether or not he realizes it, he might be pushing *you* to leave *him*."

She explained that when children are severely abused or neglected at certain critical benchmarks in their development, they generally can't sustain intimate relationships as adults, even with spouses and children they love.

"The pressure of trying can become intolerable," she told me. "I'm afraid the record isn't promising. Just being in a close relationship can trigger fear or confusion and dysfunctional reactions. Trauma survivors frequently have to detach from those they love before they can heal, especially if the loved one reminds them of their trauma."

I started to argue that I couldn't possibly remind Jay of his trauma, but that old grabby clutch in the pit of my stomach told me that my body had already absorbed the importance of her words. I wasn't his assailant. I hadn't been there when the trauma was inflicted, but he'd told me stories. Our very closeness might have turned me into someone much too close: a witness.

She spoke kindly, but kindness didn't help. I wasn't ready to know what she told me, and so I ran away.

Most years, Worth and I took a trip on our own, without our husbands, kind of a long slumber party with restaurants. It always took her weeks to figure out when she could get away from work. This time, three hours after I called her we were signed up for a tour of Vietnam. Out of a sense of duty I'd asked, "What about your clients?"

"Yeah, well," she said.

That was love.

By the end of the trip, Bea's words had sunk in. I arrived back in Boston with heavy feet and tired heart, but before I had the door fully open, Jay was there in the entryway with the lively eyes and huge smile of an earlier era, wrapping me in his arms, suitcase and all. We were goofy with new love, serene with old love, and buoyant with relief. A week passed like this. Two weeks. Yet another week. A seventeen-day separation had restored us in the nick of time.

One ordinary night, we were winding up a day as we usually did, Jay in the bedroom chair with his book, I in our bed with mine, from time to time reading passages out loud to each other. Suddenly I sensed something sulfurous in the room and looked up. Jay sat rigid, spine straight as a sword, face hard as a hitman's. I sucked in a breath and froze. His words were slow with contempt, poisoning the air as they came for me.

You are *this*, he said, his voice pounding like a fist. You are *that*.

My memory for the spoken word is prodigious, and even in that incomprehensible moment, I knew that to carry this speech into the future would be a curse. I willed his words to stop, but instead of silence I received a blessed amnesia: The words evaporated on impact, leaving no trace. Just a few moments later, of everything he said that night, I remembered only the very last.

". . . and all those times I said you were beautiful, I was lying."

– 23 –

THE WRONG CALAMITY

"**O**KA-A-AY," ONE OF THE MUSICIANS hollered. "Let's get this party going!" The square dance caller got everyone into formation, and that old barn was hopping.

It was my sixtieth birthday. Jay and I had rented the barn, hired the caterer, and booked the caller months earlier. Though Worth and I had been back from Vietnam just a few weeks and her work had piled up, she flew up from Atlanta, hoping to find Jay and me back to normal.

In a twirly eyelet skirt and bare-shoulder top, I swung left and allemanded right and kept a lot of distance between Jay and me. That awful night in the bedroom was still fresh. Jay had said his piece and walked out, and I'd slumped to my side and lain there inert, barely breathing. I could have been shot with a gun, I was that shattered.

The music stopped for dinner, and I went from table to table, talking to our guests across the room from where Jay was doing the same. When the caterer started serving, I sat down at the nearest table without looking to see where he was. He'd taken a seat three tables away, where there'd been only one empty chair. I have sixty-one photos from that party, and not one shows the two of us together.

My daughters surprised me with an album of letters and photos from well-wishers, and there were many toasts. Then Jay stood up, and somebody clinked a spoon on a glass. The room got quiet.

Jay had never been bashful about his love. Every birthday, anniversary, and Valentine's Day he gave me cards, sometimes two or three, with long, tender handwritten notes. Over the years, everyone in that room had heard him say how much I meant to him, and they all said he outdid himself that night. Several wiped their eyes as he spoke. A friend whispered in my ear, "Every woman here is a little jealous of you."

But I knew minutely every nuance of his voice, could decipher the smallest modulation, and I understood what I'd just heard. It was a tribute to a love that must be let go. It was a eulogy.

There would be one more incident, one that sounds so trivial, it's hard to believe it made all the difference. Jay and I had given Jeanie a necklace for a special occasion and had jointly written a card to go with it. Unbeknownst to me, he'd given her a different card, signed by him alone and implying the necklace was from just him. It was a fluke that I ever saw it, and I was so shaken, I called Bea.

"No," she said, "you're not making a mountain out of a molehill. This is terribly disappointing."

Bea had warned me that Jay's need to leave our marriage might very well grow stronger than his desire to stay in it. She'd told me he might be incapable of ending things and might try to get me to do it, but I hadn't believed he could break me. Now I saw that, as much as he loved the three of us, he would even try to drive a wedge between my girls and me if he had to. Jay and I were no longer walking together to get to the other side. At some point he'd turned toward the exit without me, and the space between us had gotten too big to close.

Before our marriage, I'd made extraordinary allowances because I knew Jay had suffered trauma. But I'd been wrong about his calamity. I'd thought it was Lydia's suicide and that, by the time we married, it had let go its hold on him. In fact, it was something else entirely, and we were no match for its power.

Only a few weeks after I found his card to Jeanie, Jay and I were in the living room, reading. Neither of us had turned on a light when the sun began to set, and the room was growing dusky. I lowered my book and looked at him for a long time, feeling myself grow dim as I silently said goodbye to this man who had been my source of light.

"Jay," I said.

He looked up, and there was no glow in him.

"I think we need a divorce, Jay."

Silently, he stood and walked toward me, his arms open. Silently, I stood and walked into them. In the middle of the room we held onto each other, a cracked pillar rocking back and forth in the deepening dark. More tears than we knew bodies could produce soaked our faces, our necks, our shirts.

"Thank you," he whispered.

In a Collaborative Divorce, the parties rule out litigation and settle the terms with the help of attorneys specially trained in collaborative law. Jay wanted the condo, and I quickly agreed. We easily settled the other belongings, and the four of us—Jay and me, his lawyer and mine—met to work out the rest.

At the first meeting, the lawyers pulled our prenup from their files and my stomach clenched.

Jay announced, "I'm not invoking it."

His lawyer shifted in his seat. "Ah, well, let's just take a look . . ." and Jay said firmly, "I'm waiving the prenup."

At the very moment we were solidifying our dissolution, he did what he'd done throughout the years, the unexpected thing that made me love him even more.

"Thank you," I whispered.

Dispossessed of husband, marriage, home, and the future I'd imagined, I was without landmarks. I couldn't find my way to familiar places, lost track of time and day, forgot to eat or ate double. It felt like the sea had surged in and carried off the known world.

I needed to find an apartment, but just reading the listings overwhelmed me. "Where should I live," I asked my friend Nancy, who knows everything. She'd gone through her own divorce, also a shocker, and understood the state I was in.

"This is the building you want," she said, and she gave me an address.

I went there, saw three apartments, and chose the one on the seventh floor. Later in the day I called the building manager and said actually, the one on the eleventh floor. The next morning I said no, the one on fifteen.

"This has to be final," she said.

"Yes, I'm so sorry . . . I'm not usually so . . . yes, I know . . . sorry."

Jeanie had a new job in New York and wouldn't be able to get away on my moving day. She called frequently to ask how I felt, whether I was getting enough sleep, what the new apartment was like.

"It's awful," I said. "It's tiny. Dark as a drawer. Suffocating, actually. I'm sure my stuff won't fit."

"I wish I could be there for the move," she said. "I'll come as soon as I can."

Friends came and helped me pack. They worked hard. They brought wine. They kept me anchored. Because I'd come to love it, Jay gave me a painting that had been in his family. Because he'd come to love it, I gave him pottery I'd hand-carried from Japan.

"Take whatever furniture you want," he said, and I took care to leave him ample. I asked him not to be home when I left, and he agreed, looking so sad that I almost hugged him but stopped myself, remembering just in time what all of this was about.

The day before the move, my brother Craig arrived from California to help me. That night my friend Pat called and said, "I'm leaving work at noon to help you unpack. I'll bring lunch for both of us."

"You don't have to miss work," I said. "My brother's here."

"I'll bring lunch for him too," she answered. Twenty-six years earlier, Pat had introduced me to Charlie, who'd introduced me to Jay. Now she would come bearing food to help me leave him.

Before I closed the condo door behind me, I rearranged the furniture to eliminate the empty spaces left by the pieces I was taking.

A mover carried the last carton into my new apartment and left. Only a few seconds later, my doorbell rang. "They must have forgotten something," I called to Craig and Pat. "I'll get it." But it wasn't the movers. It was Jeanie, arrived from New York even though she'd have to turn around and go back in just three hours. "Jeanie. Oh, Jeanie," was all I could manage, and I started to cry. She gave me a squeeze, then walked among the towers of boxes and surveyed the place.

"What a great apartment!" she cried. "I love it! A balcony! Look at the size of this closet! In New York this closet would be a bedroom!"

I looked up and saw that the rooms weren't dark and suffocating after all. They were sunny. A breeze came in from the balcony.

"I'm thinking the couch is in the wrong place," Jeanie said.

"It sure is," said Craig. "Let's fix that."

Fixing it, we made big bubbles in the carpet. I leaned against a wall and watched as Craig and Pat started pulling on the rug's edges to flatten them, but Jeanie grabbed both my hands and swung me around. To her bouncy oom-pah oom-pah, the two of us polkaed the carpet smooth.

The apartment was a third the size of the condo I'd just left, but all my things fit. It was fine, better than fine, for just one person. Being just one person was the thing that wasn't fine.

Alimony waiver. Done. Transfers of marital property. Done. Yet another meeting in my attorney's office to tick documents off the list. Jay and his lawyer sat at opposite ends of the small conference table. I sat catty-corner to Jay, and my lawyer sat next to me. In the middle of the meeting, a convulsion rippled through my body. I looked up quickly, but no one had noticed. The conversation receded as I tried to control what was happening inside me. I'm going to throw up! I thought, and I didn't dare try to speak. Harder and harder I fought to hold back what was coming, but I couldn't contain it. Suddenly I erupted, not with vomit but with jagged sobs.

My lawyer jumped up and grabbed a box of tissues from her desk.

Jay patted my back and said, "Doll, doll, what is it? What's wrong?"

"Let's leave them alone," my lawyer said to his, and the two of them hurried out.

I was keening and gasping for breath. Jay kept patting my back. Finally I was able to cry out, "Why is this happening? What are we doing here?"

Still patting my back, he said, "I know. I know, doll. I know."

What he didn't say was, "I know, doll. Let's get out of here. Let's go home."

– 24 –

THE OTHER SIDE

THE UNDOING OF OUR MARRIAGE took three years, and it was two times that before I was fully recomposed. In the beginning, my emotions surged fruitlessly. Fury with no target. Love with no lover. A piece of junk mail for Mr. and Mrs. made me take to my bed. The lyrics of a song on the radio—*"Don't cry young lovers because I'm alone"*—made me want to attack. *Do* cry, I silently screamed, *precisely* because I'm alone! Then, suddenly expended, I sat on my couch with erect posture, hands neatly folded in my lap, and cried for myself with strange primness.

I imagined what Jay would have said to comfort me, but without his voice, the words taunted. Friends called, and in return for their kindness I gave them dispirited silences or disjointed ramblings. After a time or two, some lay low to wait until I was easier to deal with. Though I knew not to resent this, I resented it.

A woman I barely knew phoned too often. Her husband had died around the time of our divorce, and she was intent on being the most aggrieved. "At least your man isn't dead," she told me for the third or fourth time. "You're luckier than me."

I should have just offered sympathy and let her be. Instead, I said icily, "I don't think that's a contest either of us wants to win," and I cut off her discourse on my enviable good fortune. For hours afterward, I railed at her in my head. "Your husband's love letters still ring true! Your husband isn't walking the earth, not giving you a thought!"

I'd wanted to win the contest after all.

I grieved that when Jay and I were in our last good years, I hadn't known the end was coming and so hadn't committed to memory the last time we'd laughed out loud together, slow-danced in the kitchen, slept like tangled vines. Might I possibly have done something to change the future? I lost scores, maybe hundreds, of hours of sleep to this question.

I had no happy memories. None. Jay's face, the first time we woke up together. As soon as I recalled it, that endearing face grimaced and twisted into Warrior's. A photo of the two of us in a crowd of cousins, his arm around my shoulders, both of us shining. "You're so beautiful," he'd said a moment earlier. "We need a picture." That photo had always evoked in me the bliss of a special night. Now it brought forth no feelings, just the coldhearted facts—the occasion, the location. It could have been a picture in someone else's album.

While the good memories perished, the bad ones stood firm, his final screed in the bedroom most of all. The night of the gun is how I thought of it. We weren't gun people. There hadn't been a gun. Still, to me it was the night of the gun.

"He might not be able to pull the trigger," Bea had warned me, but that night he'd been more than able. I'd seen him clearly. His eyes had been undeniably locked on mine; both his forearms manifestly pressed down hard on the arms of the chair, knuckles white from gripping the edges. And even though I knew this, even while I saw this, I could see his hands aiming a gun, his eye squinting through the sight, his finger working the trigger.

You are *this*, and a bullet destroyed my will to hear.

You are *that*, and my hope bled out.

And all those times I said you were beautiful . . . My heart! It ruptured.

And it wasn't just the gun. Unbearable images of what Jay's parents had done to him still replayed in my mind. Little-boy Jay, abused and assaulted while I was compelled to watch but unable to intervene, both of us being tortured.

I'd lost the future we'd envisioned, and now, stripped of the happy memories and festering with the bad ones, I lost the good past too. Nothing but the worst remained. I could hardly walk for the sorrow of it.

Winter was upon us, and I found I couldn't trust the universe. I'd always loved snugging in during snowstorms, but now I worried that a snowplow would lose its traction and come crashing through the wall.

Stuck in a box in the back of a closet, the fur hat Jay bought me was now just an extravagant hat owned by a non-extravagant woman. I took it to one furrier, and then a second, hoping something could be done with it. That hat could only be what that hat was, they told me. Not a headband. Not a collar.

"Most women would be thrilled to have a hat like this," said one.

"You should put it on and strut," said the other.

But I didn't want a trophy hat. All I wanted was a modest memento, a small furry thing to remind me in the cold that most of our years had been good ones, when he'd warmed my winters and I'd warmed his.

My books were shelved, my pictures hung, and still my new apartment felt like somewhere I didn't belong. Only when I was at work with Jay and Hojun and the rest of our team did I feel centered and purposeful. Jay and I automatically left our personal problems behind when we went to the office, and none of our colleagues sensed our troubles. Two months before I moved out of the condo, Jay and I privately told Hojun we were breaking up. His face wilted with the news, reviving a bit only when we told him that, as he'd seen, the two of us could still work together well, and we wanted to. The three of us agreed that, after the divorce, Jay's and my roles would continue unchanged, and we sealed the deal with a three-way hug.

By six weeks after I'd moved out of the condo, Jay and I had settled all the terms of our divorce except some final financial details. Our lawyers had tried to be helpful, but it became clear that their efforts weren't moving us forward. One night, when Hojun and the others had left for the evening, the two of us stayed late at the office to try to resolve these last items on our own.

With what felt reassuringly familiar and touchingly like affection, we found we still had our openness to each other and the will to find a solution that satisfied us both. It was midnight when we sent an email to our lawyers. "Good news!" it said, as though we were announcing a reconciliation.

Two weeks later, we filed our divorce papers.

Three months after that, I was fired.

Jay and Hojun had stopped by my desk and invited me to go out to lunch with them. They delivered the news in the restaurant.

"It was all my decision," said Hojun. "Given your marital . . . the situation . . . I was . . . I would feel uncomfortable if we were all. . . . Jay had nothing to do with it."

Jay's expressionless eyes watched Hojun. Hojun's eyes looked down. Jay took over to make sure I understood that the decision was final. Another trigger had needed pulling, and his fixer had buckled.

The waiter arrived with our order just as I stood up and gathered my things. All three of them looked baffled.

"At least stay and eat with us," Hojun said.

"Whatever for?" I said acidly, and I walked out.

I was dismantled. In one blow, just five months after losing my marriage, my home, and my way of being, I lost my professional status, my colleagues, my salary, the stimulation of working hard and making a difference—my reasons to get out of bed in the morning. I'd also lost my link to the one thing Jay and I had seemed to retain: the uncomplicated harmony with which we worked together.

Walking out on that lunch was hardly a grand gesture, but it was at least a trace of backbone at a time when I had no fight in me. There was no one to be angry with but Jay, and that anger I wouldn't allow. When Bea said that the nature of his trauma might force him to break away from loved ones in order to heal, I took her seriously. I wouldn't blame Jay for letting me go, any more than I'd blame someone with dementia for forgetting my name.

"Pretty noble of you," snorted Worth, "considering you're a victim too."

"I know," I said, all cool and reasonable, "but not as much as Jay is. Anyway, he *had* to push me away. It's the PTSD. Bea said so."

"You'd moved out. You'd filed your divorce papers. What was left to push? And if he found he couldn't keep working with you after all, why didn't he talk to you privately? Honestly, couldn't he have shown some regret? Some kindness? A little respect?"

I had no answer. The truth is, I was so furious with Jay I felt wired with explosives that could blow at any provocation. I couldn't admit this rage to anyone, especially to myself. Come hell or high water, I would be my best self and not blame the victim.

I operated to a tidy story of what had happened to us: Jay and I deeply loved each other. We were happily married for years, and then long-buried memories of childhood trauma came to get him. All we wanted was to make it through that terrible time together, but it was too much to want. We'd been our best selves in our marriage, and we were our best selves in our breakup, taking care of each other even as we pulled apart.

Such a powerhouse, that little narrative. No wonder I held on to it so tightly. It confirmed that our marriage hadn't been a mistake; that we'd been collateral damage, caught up in something terrible and beyond our control. It was romantic, affecting, self-congratulatory, and even true.

But it wasn't the whole truth. It handily omitted the fact that soon after we separated, Jay had a girlfriend.

When someone accidentally gave me the news, I couldn't speak or move. I don't remember how that call ended. Jay and I had been apart just six months. I was still living in some liminal space between married and unmarried and so raw that the word ex-husband made my eyes well. Jay with another woman? He wasn't grieving like I was? He wasn't going to just call to say I love you? The betrayal deboned me.

Now what, I thought bitterly, do I make of *this*, Bea? *Doctor* Bea? Doctor *He-Loves-You-But-Can't-Handle-A-Relationship* Bea?

"He was so miserable when you broke up," his sister-in-law later told me. "I couldn't bear it." And she'd introduced him to a friend of a friend, who became this girlfriend.

"She isn't really a girlfriend," the Kramers said. "She and Jay, they're not like you two were. This is about companionship, that's all."

I hated them all—Jay, his sister-in-law, the Kramers—all of them who so casually swapped me out for some other woman. A voice inside me said, You may never understand this, but you *will* be able to live with it. Put it away until you're sturdier.

That was more than I could manage, but I came close. Only when someone else mentioned her did I recall that Jay had a girlfriend, and then I remembered so fleetingly, there was no time for feelings.

I'd almost entirely shut down my consulting practice to work with Jay and Hojun, and it took until my second year of being unmarried to build up my client base again. I was socializing by then too. It probably looked to everyone as though I'd moved on, but my spirit was heavy. At a funny movie with Pat, I noticed everyone was laughing except me, and it struck me that I hadn't laughed since a good two years before my divorce.

And my world was getting smaller. Marina, my Russian friend from the blizzard and probable distant relative, died of a brain tumor. Other friends moved out of town. A few couples Jay and I had been close to drifted away now that I was single, or maybe I simply wasn't good company. I sighed a lot. I was sluggish. I wanted to answer the phone and hear, "Hi, doll."

Another year passed. Jay left Boston and moved to the West Coast to live with his girlfriend. As the little voice inside me had predicted, I could live with it. Ellen was married and home with children. Jeanie was working in New York and about to get married.

"How would you feel if Jay came to the wedding?" she asked. "If it'll be hard for you, I won't invite him."

Jay had been a wonderful stepfather when we were married and remained so after our divorce. I wanted to please her, and I also wanted to show her that despite the way she'd seen her father act when I left him, there could be mutual respect after breakups.

"Of course invite Jay," I said immediately. Even as I spoke, I examined myself for a clench in my stomach and was gratified not to find one. Now I went a step further. It was time for me to acknowledge the woman Jay had met after our separation, to call her by her name and give her due regard. They'd been together almost four years. "Jay and Arlene are a couple," I told her. "You should invite them both."

I saw them come into the reception hall and went to greet them. "Hi, Arlene," I said, and I held out my hand. "I'm Marsha. It's so good to meet you." Jay and I did a quick friend-hug. What lovely flowers, such a special day, don't the kids look happy. Another quickie hug, and I moved on to other guests. There would still be times when the fact that Jay and Arlene were together would send a spasm through me, but that day wasn't one of them.

In the Barnes & Noble cafe, a woman one table over was energetically reciting into her phone her ex-husband's sins. My friend Nancy put down her cup and murmured, "Dick and I raised five kids together, and now I can't remember being married to him."

Dick was a dick who sixteen years earlier had come home one day and started slinging shirts into a suitcase.

"Another business trip?" Nancy asked. "Where to this time?"

"I have to concentrate," he said, grabbing his Grecian Formula, and she let him be.

With his suitcase in one hand and a book of hers in the other, Dick ran out the front door, stuck his head back in, and yelled, "I won't be back. I'm moving in with Eloise."

Slam. A thirty-year marriage, over.

Three weeks later, he escorted to their son's wedding the twenty-something Eloise, his secretary, whom his kids had begged him not to bring—his kids had begged, not Nancy, because Nancy was in pieces. The first time she left her house after Dick ran off was to have her hair done for their son's rehearsal dinner. She'd been crying so much, she kept her sunglasses on even during the shampoo.

Now, sitting in a coffee shop all these years later, she couldn't remember being in that marriage. The instant she said this, I realized I couldn't remember being married to Peter, either. Sure, I knew I'd married him. I remembered the portentous blizzard, the desecrated wedding cake, the Amazon, Japan, the things he did to the girls and me when I left him. But the day-to-day marriage itself? That was lost to me. What had we talked about in the evenings? How had we juggled the tiny bathroom when we got ready for work? What was our weekend routine? So different was I from the person I'd been in that marriage, I couldn't picture myself back there.

Not long after this conversation with Nancy, I woke up one morning feeling rickety and in need of pampering. I brewed the last of the special coffee, a gift from Worth, and then got annoyed with myself for drinking it without noticing. In the afternoon, my doorbell rang. It was a workman with a bucket of tools, there to finish a repair. Usually he stepped right in, booming, "Let's get to it!" but that day his eyes flicked away in careful not-looking, and he stayed outside. I looked down and saw that I'd never finished dressing. I was in jeans and a negligee.

Eventually, I connected my distraction to the previous day's news: Peter was in a coma. He'd had a cerebral hemorrhage and likely wouldn't survive the night. A few hours later, there'd come a new prognosis. He wouldn't die, but there might be brain damage. My mind snapped to the young travel buff who'd darted like a silverfish before I registered the reality of a man in his seventies with a ventilator tube down his throat.

His obsession with me had long ago run its course, and I'd borne no grudge for years. I accepted that while others had seen it plainly, I'd been singularly oblivious to the fact that when we married, he was already sliding into an off-kilter world.

I'd come to feel some empathy even toward his mother. I couldn't forgive her for everything, but I could at least understand what might have driven her. "You need to learn how to live with an extraordinary man," she'd told me. Blanche was eagle-eyed, sharp, and intensely attached to her son. How terrified she must have been by what she saw developing in him. When I walked out on him and his extraordinariness, making me a villain might have been the only way she could cope with his malady.

Now she was gone, and Peter was in the ICU and unreachable. We'd been divorced almost forty years. We weren't friends; we weren't enemies. We simply no longer figured into each other's lives. Still, we'd witnessed and shaped each other. We'd shared a history, much of it bad, some of it good, and all of it part of who we'd each been and had since become.

I was flooded with questions I didn't know I had. Where was that invisible break in the foliage that led us to the tiny boardwalk in the rainforest, to the giant vines and the birds that sparkled like jewels? I'd never thought to ask, and now I urgently wanted to know. Then came the second wash of questions. What was up with that private phone? Why did he call the cops on me?

A few weeks earlier, in a cafe with Nancy, forgetting the details of my life with Peter had struck me as a curiosity. Now it made me anxious. I wanted to retrieve from him what I realized were missing pieces of my own life, but they'd become unobtainable.

I paid dearly for attaching myself to Peter, but it's also true that when I met him, I was naive, incurious, timid, and provincial. With him, I'd become an urbanite, someone who loved big cities, had lived abroad, and had come to understand that many of the things I'd learned growing up were all just possibilities, and not necessarily the best.

Under his influence, I'd become a person who'd jump at the chance to go to a jungle.

— 25 —

REVELATIONS

T HE NIGHT THE REVELATION CAME, I had dinner plans. That morning, I'd researched cars and decided on a Hyundai to replace my old Camry. In the afternoon, I'd looked through the Boston University catalog and selected a course to take in the fall. Around 5:00, I drove to my friend Betsy's. Pat was already there, and Betsy walked us around and showed us the work she'd done on her house and garden. Then we caravanned in our three cars to have dinner at Isabella, a good neighborhood place a couple towns over. The maître d' led us to a table in a quiet corner, and we sipped our drinks while we decided what to order.

"The tortellini looks good," Pat said casually.

"I'm going to New York," I said, equally casually.

"Nice," said Betsy, still looking at the menu. "This weekend? To see Jeanie?"

"No," I said. "For good. I'm moving there."

Pat jerked back in her seat. Betsy was shocked and a bit indignant. "You're what? You're leaving us?"

Only I was unruffled—surprisingly unsurprised, considering I'd had no idea I was even contemplating a move, much less that I'd be announcing it that evening. As soon as I heard my own words, though, I knew my New York plans as I knew my own birthday, not as news but as settled fact. Without having to stop and think, I was ready with fully formed answers to every question they asked. When would I go? In October, four months away. Did I know anyone there besides Jeanie? No. I'd ask friends and family to introduce me to their New York friends. Would I take my car? No. I'd sell it.

Good thing I hadn't ordered that Hyundai.

After more than forty years in Boston, I left for New York City in October, right on plan. For a few years afterwards, I found myself unaccountably gloomy and, like clockwork, laid low with bronchitis every October. I hadn't realized it at the time, but my move to New York was just a few days after the fifth anniversary of my separation from Jay and five days shy of what would have been our eighteenth wedding anniversary. Both the gloominess and the bronchitis ended once I put two and two together.

Jeanie had a baby, and Jay flew in for the celebration. He'd been renting out our Boston condo since moving in with Arlene, and he brought with him some papers he needed me to sign so he could sell it. We went to a notary and then out to lunch.

At the restaurant he held the door for me, as I knew he would. I asked for a booth, as he knew I would. Like riding a bike.

"You look good."

"You do too."

"My life is tranquil now," he said. "The West Coast suits me."

"I'm glad I moved to New York," I said. "It's the perfect place for me."

On our way back to Jeanie's, standing on a corner, waiting for the light to change, I said what mattered most.

"I'm glad we were married," I said. "I'm a better person because of you. I would do it again, even knowing the ending."

"Oh, doll," he said. "Me too. So much." And we hugged on the sidewalk in the bright June sun, looking for all the world like a pair of lovers.

In that redemptive moment, I felt a sense of peace I hadn't felt since our divorce. Warrior, the night of the gun, even the shock of learning that Jay had a girlfriend—those memories were defanged. Now I could remember the goodness of what we'd shared. I was myself again, not the same self I'd been when we were married, but an intact, sturdy self, able to have a good life, even with a deeply sad event in my past.

A year later, I was pulling a warm jumble of towels from the dryer when a burst of images exploded in front of me and coalesced into a scene from the past. "Did you sign this of your own free will?" a judge is asking. "Yes," I answer woodenly, and with that, our divorce papers are filed. Jay and I leave the courthouse and head for our separate cars.

It's been only eight weeks since I moved out of our condo, and I'm still floundering. My head is boggy. The walkway between the courthouse and the parking lot seems longer than it was an hour earlier and cratered with potholes that I'm sure weren't there before. I'm struggling to walk and not certain I'll make it to my car.

"I have to confess something to you," Jay says. He is walking easily. "I told my kids that a lot of things were your fault."

I'm dulled and depleted, not up to new information, but with a reflexive responsiveness to him that is no longer useful, I ask, "Things like what?"

"Like, if they invited us to visit," he says, "I'd say I wanted to but had to check with you. Then I'd call them back without telling you about it and say you'd said no. Things like that."

I don't turn to him in fury. I don't demand that he call his kids and set the record straight. I don't even say, "The whole time? From the very start?" He may or may not want forgiveness, but I don't inquire. I simply give it to him, like someone unaware that she's been sold out.

"Never mind. It's history now," I say, and I focus on navigating the potholes.

And here, six years later, in a laundry room two hundred miles from that courthouse parking lot, his confession breaks through to my consciousness and I'm thunderstruck by my lapdog pardon. I want him to confess again. Right now! Looking me in the eye! I want details! I want justice!

It hits me suddenly that I've been ambushed by a memory I myself buried to make it through a divorce caused by memories Jay buried. The irony enrages me.

But as quickly as it bubbled up, my rage boiled off. Calmly, I folded the towels. I didn't need Jay to confess again. I didn't need the details. How could I, of all people, not look at his lies with compassion? A grant, not a loan, I'd told the financial aid officer; a widow, not a divorcée, I'd said to my landlady. Nothing I'd dealt with in my own life had come close to what he'd endured; even so, when I'd felt cornered, I lied myself to safety.

With the benefit of much time gone by, I accepted that he'd lied and tried to understand why. I couldn't believe that the Jay I'd married would lie to me, but, of course, he wasn't the Jay I'd married. He was a man gutted by unimaginable revelations.

When he started recovering his memories, Jay insisted we not tell his kids anything about his revealed past, a decision I thought then and think today was entirely his to make. At about that same time, his children started having children of their own. We were loony in love with those babes, and we thought his kids were warming to our marriage because of this. Perhaps, I mused, his kids' new openness, just when he needed more distance, was more than he could take, and so he lied about me to push them back to their original position.

Or maybe he lied so his kids would convince *him* to leave *me*. Certainly, they'd have been happy to oblige. Perhaps their hostility didn't stem from loyalty to their late mother after all, but rather from an instinctive awareness that there were family secrets that had to be kept hidden, and that a newcomer to their tightly guarded world might poke around and bring them to light.

With a strong dose of self-comfort, I even considered the possibility that he hadn't lied to his kids at all but told me he had so I'd feel well rid of him.

I could make a case for these and half a dozen other possibilities for why Jay might have lied, but the truth was it no longer mattered. Recalling his confession gave me something much more valuable: self-exoneration. In our darkening living room six years earlier, in a moment that had everything riding on it, I'd said, "I think we need a divorce, Jay." I'd anguished ever since over whether I'd made a terrible mistake. Might we have made it to the other side together if I'd tried harder, softer, smarter, subtler, fiercer, gentler, longer, kinder?

Now I understood that I hadn't ended a marriage that might have survived. I'd ended my own fiction that its center was still holding.

A revelation can simply spring from nowhere in the middle of dinner? I wanted the how of it. How had my brain, without my awareness, figured out that I should move to New York? How had all the details just come to me, as though planted under hypnosis? I carried these questions to New York, and, three years later, I met someone in my neighborhood I thought could answer them. He was a doctor, a scientist, and I wanted science, words like *latent* and *dendrites* and *prefrontal cortex*. I had a notebook.

He listened with keen attention to my account of that dinner at Isabella. Encouraged by his concentration, I offered up every detail, right down to Pat's tortellini. When I finished, I could see his mind working, putting it all together. I waited expectantly, pen in hand.

"I think," he said finally, "that you have a little someone within you who's always on your side."

I put away my notebook.

– 26 –

FINDING MY FOOTING

A LITTLE SOMEONE WITHIN ME. I called her Claire, a name
that sounds like a bell and means clear or bright. Before I
could look out for myself, Claire was already there and trying
hard to help me. By the quicksand in Canada, she tried to get
my attention, but I didn't know how to see her. When I didn't
just say no to Peter's proposal, she flashed me the image of that
listless couple in a loveless living room. Still, I ignored her,
and so she showed me something worse, a vision of myself in a
coffin. When even with that I said yes, I would marry him, it
must have flattened her.

But she rallied. When the humiliation of Peter's private
phone paralyzed me, it was Claire who spurred me to action,
who told me to knuckle down and lose weight, to change
myself because I couldn't change *him*; Claire who, clear as a
bell, told me to pick up my daughter and leave Japan, with or
without him; who pushed me into my father's truck before I'd
consciously understood that I mustn't spend even one more
night with a man who'd set the cops on me.

After a while, though, I started asking myself troublesome questions. If Claire could get me to lose weight, couldn't she have kept me from gaining it in the first place? If she could push me into a truck to get away from Peter, couldn't she have pushed me away from him at the very beginning? Claire, I concluded, simply hadn't measured up. Did I really have to spend years feeling worthless, eating compulsively, and absorbing my parents' disdain as gospel?

Yes. I did.

To my mother, I was a no-account. My father recoiled from me. In my child's heart, each proved the other right: I was someone who didn't matter. I believed this because believing their parents is what children do. Of course I reacted in primitive ways to the pain of it. I was just a child, and so was Claire. Between us, we did the best we could. Obsessive eating was a flawed analgesic, but it brought at least momentary relief from the shame of being unnecessary.

I used to look back to those early days and chafe at my young self's bad choices. Now I say to that girl, You avoided the worst paths, the ones with no return. With only a child's tools to work with, you gave yourself enough comfort to keep moving forward and imposed on yourself only consequences you could later manage. You did well, little one.

Forty years ago, my lawyer's frustration when I kept talking about the Japanese teacups confused me. Now I get it. Those teacups were irrelevant, was her point. Avoiding jail was a relief, but it wasn't the end of the story. How could I not see that Peter was intent on vengeance, she wanted to know.

Didn't I realize I had to do more than just wait for his next bad thing?

I'd looked at her and shrugged. No matter how much she tried to get me to open my eyes, I couldn't see myself as someone who'd ever be able to handle things. What I didn't yet know is that the ability to handle things had been in me from the start. Call it selfhood, call it grit, call it agency or resilience—every once in a while, I still call her Claire. All she needed was someone to nurture and develop her. My parents weren't up to it, but to my great fortune, there were people around me who stepped in. Rabbi Steve and DeeDee Weisberg, who got me to leave a place where I wasn't thriving. Sol, who took a chance on me at Mattel. Frieda, who asked why I stayed with Peter and propelled me into business school. Lydia, who fought to get me $1,500. My professors, who didn't flunk me. Anne, who didn't kick me out. And from day one, there were my grandparents.

Bill and Julia, my mother's parents, were born in America to families of means and lived in comfort in Indiana. Max and Minnie, my father's parents, fled pogroms and lived a life of sufficiency in New York. What these two couples had in common were happy marriages fortified with unresented compromise. They also had in common the pain and puzzlement of discovering that the son and daughter they'd raised, my parents, were committed only to themselves and fortified by their grievances.

All I had to do to make my grandmothers, Minnie and Julia, happy was walk into the room. These women loved, taught, and protected me in ways that went far beyond tuition checks or a trunk full of home cooking.

When my grandmother Julia came to visit, I sheltered at her side. On one occasion, when I was fourteen, my mother went out, and my grandmother and I settled in for conversation. As always, she sat in the big green chair by the picture window, and I sat on the floor, at her feet, holding her right hand and turning her wedding ring around and around on her finger. She'd been a widow for four years and would live another fifteen, dismissing two would-be suitors and wearing that ring until the day she died.

I can't remember what we were talking about, but when she suddenly said, "I don't know why she's like this," it didn't fit with our conversation. I looked up and saw her gazing into the distance. "We gave her everything she wanted," she said to the air in front of her. "We did everything we could for her, Bill." I was riveted. She was in some kind of trance, talking to her long-buried husband, my grandfather. As she poured her heart out, it became clear she was talking about my mother. I didn't move, terrified of breaking the spell.

"And our Marsha," she said. "She's mean to her, Bill. It breaks my heart." I froze. Of course I knew my mother was always mad at me, but the notion that her anger was meanness? That startled me, and I forgot myself.

"Mom's mean?" I asked.

Her body jolted. "What?"

"You said Mom's mean. How is she mean?"

Obviously flustered, she fluttered her hands in front of her face and said, "I didn't say a thing. I was just thinking about your Grandpa Bill." She stood and left the room.

On the last day of her visit, she pulled me into my bedroom and closed the door. "There's nothing wrong with you," she whispered. "You're fine. Do you understand?" It would take years, but eventually I did.

There was no such dramatic incident with my grandmother Minnie. Except for when we briefly lost each other when my mother took me off to Indiana, she was always looking out for me. Even at two or three I understood this; I nagged for sleepovers at her apartment and usually prevailed. When I was four or five, she was the one who taught me to wash my hands after using the bathroom, something my parents had omitted when they got me out of diapers. "This is one way big girls take care of themselves," she told me, and I felt myself blooming as I solemnly soaped each finger.

When I was in first grade, she started asking me what I was reading. For two years, I proudly bragged about my *Dick and Jane* level. "But what are you reading at home?" she invariably asked, and my invariable answer was, "Nothing." My mother read only "women's magazines," and I never saw my father read. From where I sat, books were for school.

In third grade, I came home one day and found a package waiting for me on the dining room table. Wrapped in brown paper, bearing five stamps and tied with string, it came from Minnie. Inside, with no note or inscription, was a small green book, *The Bobbsey Twins, or Merry Days, Inside and Out*. It wasn't a book for today's sensibilities, but it did what she'd hoped. Those twins and their merry days had me by page two. I chewed through their adventures, and soon *The Bobbsey Twins in the Country* arrived. Then *The Bobbsey Twins at Snow Lodge . . . on a Houseboat . . . in a Great City*. After forty-two volumes of Bobbseys, the Nancy Drews started coming, and I was hooked by this canny "girl detective" and her blue roadster. I'd become a reader. Thirty years later, reading Toni Morrison's *Beloved,* I came upon the words, "Love is or it ain't. Thin love ain't no love at all." How thick Grandma Minnie's love was.

Sadly, both my grandfathers died young. Minnie's husband, Max, was debilitated by two strokes before I had a chance to really know him; Bill I knew mostly from summer visits, when I was very young and still living in New Jersey with both my parents. By the time I was old enough to form sharp memories of him, he was already slowed by the bad heart that would kill him. I do, though, have a clear memory of the day I first felt brave. I was seven, and it was because of Bill.

We were visiting my grandparents in Indiana, and seemingly overnight, the Brood X cicadas emerged in Lafayette. The sidewalks were terrifying. Bill swooped me up, and so softly that I had to stop crying to hear him, he whispered into my ear the astonishing lifecycle of the red-eyed invaders whose sounds had taken over the air and whose empty shells crunched sickeningly under our shoes.

"I'm not afraid anymore, Grandpa," I'm told I said. "You can put me down on my own feet."

So hard was it to be my mother's daughter, it took me years to acknowledge that going back home at thirty-three to an illiberal town where everyone knew her business must have felt cruelly different from the triumphant return she'd imagined when she left my father. I see now that she might very well have resented her life. What I don't understand is how that resentment got directed at me, especially when I was so very young.

As for my father, fifteen years ago he cut off all ties with me, enlisting someone else to deliver that news by email. "Your father feels that you may be more of your mother's daughter than you had hoped for," the email said. Almost fifty years after their divorce and six years after her death, he was still fighting my mother and still seeing me as her surrogate. He wouldn't answer my calls, letters, or emails. I've lost any desire for reconnecting, and that feels like growth.

I don't know what drove either of them to act as they did, but I know for certain that they strongly influenced my own approach to parenthood. They did this by demonstrating how I mustn't be. It's a sad way to learn, but it's not nothing.

By the time I married Jay, I was self-aware and emotionally strong—someone who could handle things. When our marriage ended, squalls of grief flung me back to a time when I'd felt inept. I lost my way in familiar territory; didn't trust my judgment; felt sometimes hollow, sometimes like solid lead; waited passively for the next bad thing. My dormant eating disorder returned, and I gained thirty pounds without realizing. Yes, without realizing.

It had taken me maybe twenty-five years to evolve from the vulnerable person my parents reared to a sure-footed woman standing on the foundation erected by my grandparents and others who'd believed in me. My relapse was crushing, but that hard-earned sure-footedness proved to be durable: It took nowhere near another twenty-five years to regain it.

That happened almost imperceptibly. At one point, I was sorting old photos and realized Jay's face wasn't morphing into Warrior's. At other points, I realized I was eating properly, socializing, engaging fully in my work, making solid decisions, able to laugh again, able to feel joy.

Ten years ago, while waiting for a light to change on a corner near Jeanie's house, Jay and I told each other that we were glad we'd been married, that we'd do it again, even knowing the ending. We'd hugged on the sidewalk, looking for all the world like a couple of lovers, which we weren't.

We saw each other again about a year ago. We met for dinner and talked for hours, only briefly speaking of our bad times, both of us now past them. Easily, naturally, uncomplicatedly, we fell into the kind of rich conversation that had been our way. Like riding a bike.

At the end of the evening we told each other, If you're ever in trouble, just call; we'll stay in touch; we won't wait such a long time to get together again. We hugged goodbye, looking for all the world like old friends. Which maybe we are. Time will tell. Despite our intentions, in the aftermath of that evening we emailed only a couple of times.

I never pine for Jay anymore. The hole in my heart where he used to be healed over years ago. Occasionally I miss having that special closeness with someone, and then the scar might tug. A friend, on her sixtieth birthday, said ruefully, "At our age, everyone has something chronic." Perhaps this is mine. If so, I've gotten off easy.

ACKNOWLEDGMENTS

Ever since the day she first tossed me a note in high school, Barbara Worth Ratner has been my world-expanding, straight-shooting, huge-hearted sidekick and inspiration through thick, thin, and durian.

Steve Gross saw this book coming before I did, generously read more drafts than was fair of me to ask, and unfailingly got me back on the right road whenever I wrote myself into a dead end.

Joyce Johnson insisted that my work should be a memoir, not the collection of personal essays I'd intended. I resisted. Thank goodness she persisted.

Many thanks to Gordon McClelland, who embraced this book from the start, and to the entire team at DartFrog Books for their talent and drive.

Both Peter and Jay knew I was writing this memoir and warmly supported it. I'm indebted to each of them for providing important details and filling in gaps in my memory.

Anoushka Sinha's confidence and insightful feedback got me going again when I'd come to a stop. Marcia Biederman, Karen Gray Ruelle, Christine Yared, and the rest of our Tuesday authors group provided wisdom and soul-filling sisterhood.

Long before I started writing, back when I was living the story this book recounts, the late Rabbi Stephen Weisberg and his wife, DeeDee, cared for me in ways both crucial and kind. Craig Davis, Joyce Bohnen, Pat Baillieul, Phyllis Cohen, Jeffrey Lazarus, and Nancy Korman appeared like magic to help me over hurdles I couldn't manage on my own.

At Harvard Business School, Richard Malavenda and other first-year sectionmates steadfastly looked out for me. Bringing class notes to the Stillman Infirmary and pushing me around campus in a whack-a-doodle wheelchair might have seemed like nothing to them, but to me it was everything.

Finally, there are others in my heart and in my story who aren't here to see this book come to be. I offer up my immense gratitude and honor the memories of Minnie Lerner Davis, Max Davis, Julia Benjamin Zimmerman, William Zimmerman, Robert Dalton, Ed Simon, Frieda Ployer, Sol Mester, Marina Yampolsky, Dr. William Kaden, Anne Kates, Lil Little, Mel Miller, Mildred Miller, and Marjorie Hirsh.

DISCUSSION QUESTIONS

- What were the underlying forces that made Marsha agree to marry Peter despite knowing the marriage would "nail her into a very bad box"? What, if any, decisions have you made that you later realized were made for the wrong reasons?

- Marsha lied to the business school financial aid officer about her loan and to her landlady about being divorced. What would you have done in her place?

- Some people might say Marsha was a fool for running from the police or trying to go to work in a deadly blizzard. Others might say she was resourceful or naive. What would you say?

- Marsha told Jay, "I'm glad we were married. I'm a better person because of you." What do you think she meant by "a better person," and why did she credit Jay?

- How did you react to the sudden appearance of Claire? Why do you think Marsha gave her a name? When, if ever, have you had a "Claire" in your life?

- What are your observations about the role of memories and their impact on the arc of this book?

- Marsha tells us, "By the time I married Jay, I was self-aware and emotionally strong—someone who could handle things." Do you agree or disagree? What were some of the stumbling blocks and steppingstones of her evolution over time?

- What were your initial feelings about Peter and Jay? How did these feelings change over the course of the book?

- How did you react to the last four paragraphs of the book? Did you expect—or want—a different ending?

- What does the title, *The Wrong Calamity*, mean to you?

- What incidents in the book did you particularly respond to? What lessons or inspirations from this book will you carry with you?

- If you had the opportunity to speak with her, what would you want to ask or tell Marsha?

ABOUT THE AUTHOR

Having grown up in a small Midwest town, Marsha Jacobson went to college in Boston and discovered she's a city gal. She now lives in New York City and is an author, teacher, and writing coach. Her work has appeared in the *New York Times*; the *Visible Ink* anthology; and the flash fiction anthology, *For Sale: Baby Shoes, Never Worn*. Her memoir, *The Wrong Calamity*, is her debut book. Previously, she was an executive in corporations and nonprofits and a consultant to nonprofits. When she's not writing, you might find her reading in a park or cooking something out of the ordinary in her kitchen while singing along with a playlist.